I Am A Disabled Veteran

Delcha P. Williams

ISBN: 0615469043
ISBN-13: 9780615469041

The book is dedicated to my Mother, Father,
Brother and Nephew.
They held in there as long as they could
But became tired
And
Went to sleep and never woke up

Vallerie Idel Williams
Odis Williams
Robert Jerome Stepter
Robert Jerome Stepter Jr.

May God Bless Their Soles

CONTENT

ACKNOWLEDGEMENT

I would personally like to thank the men and women in the Armed Services who put themselves in danger to protect our country and the less fortunate across the world.

Please take care of yourselves. Your families want you back safe and sound As Soon As Possible.

My name is Del Williams. I am a 53 years old Disabled Veteran previously rated at 40% combined rating for cold injuries to my lower extremities. As of June 2010, I received a 90% combined rating but was classified as 100% unemployable by the Veterans Administration (VA). This rating allowed me to receive full disability compensation benefits from the VA. The process of acquiring my unemployable status took up the past ten years of my life, but at the end I received the majority of what I was seeking. I am currently working on an appeal for injuries that I still feel were secondary, caused or aggravated by my service related conditions, which were denied by the Rating Board and I am seeking higher individual rating for those conditions that the VA felt were caused by my service connected injuries.

Within this book you will be educated on the do's and don'ts on how to apply and possibly secure your disability or pension compensation. I will attempt to keep it as simple as possible.

I will not be going into a long drawn out history on compensation but rather my goal is to inform you in a clear and detailed manner on how to submit a file that will greatly increase your chances of receiving compensation. To inform you on anything other than that would be a waste of your time as well as mine. There are many books out there that show you what forms to fill out and then tell you to send your supporting documents with it. That's all in good, but there is a lot more to it than just submitting medical documents and forms. You need to know where to look and how to intrepid the laws that governs disability and pension compensation.

You will learn the proper verbiage to use in your letters to the Rating Board; what to place in your submission file, as well as how to package your new, higher rating or appeal case file in order to greater your chances for receiving monetary benefits. You will also be educated on applying for a 100% disability or unemployability ratings. It is easy to find out what VA forms are needed to apply but you need to learn; what to say and how to word it on these forms, how should your supporting medical documents read and what is the Rating Board looking for when they read your records. Additionally, within this reading there could be information that you may or may not know of referencing additional monetary gains and/or support from the VA after you have been successfully rated such as, being able to recuperate co-payments that you made on medication from the first day you submitted your case file to the VA. If you are rated 50% or higher, medication from the VA is free. This means that upon successfully acquiring at least a 50% rating, you are eligible to receive back all of the copayments that you made to the VA from the date the VA stated you became disabled at a 50% or higher rating.

If you have a Service Representative (SR), a person authorized and/or employed by the VA to assist veterans with their compensation cases and/or other programs, this is a good thing. A SR will be able to verify the information that I am about to explain to you. If you do not have a SR get one. You do not have to take on the VA on your own, especially when there are knowledgeable and competent individuals that can assist you for free. Though I completely did my own case, I do not recommend anyone to do this without some form of assistance. I eventually obtained a SR during the last year of my appeals case but by then I had already submitted all documentation and the Rating Board was in the final stages of completing my case. I began to become burned out and if I was going to have to go through a longer period of time dealing with the Rating Board, I wanted to get help to take some of the stress off of me. *My trials and errors are going to help you tremendously.* SR's are there to help you, so let them. The majority of SR's have seen or been directly involved with a hearing through the Rating Board and are well informed as to their procedures and policies. Bear in mind the SR is an employee who works eight hours a day five days per week. Some take their work home when it comes to helping Vets prepare their claims when going before an appeals board at a specific date but in general their weekends are personal days, so do not expect them to work with you on weekends. Though the SR can help with acquiring VA medical files and through the entire submission process, I am going to ask you to obtain private and VA medical records and other supporting documents on your own behalf, which will be submitted with your file. It is your responsibility to make sure you get your benefits. This will also give you the opportunity to actually read all of your medical records to make sure they have the necessary information within them. I personally read every private and VA medical record I have which extended all the way back through my military career to the present. I was going to make sure (1) that I understood what each physician said about my condition and (2) does the information in the records contain the required etiology of my service related medical conditions. If I did not understand something, I would ask my primary doctor to explain it in laymen terms. You will see why this is important later in the book.

Over the past ten plus years, I educated myself on all the rules and regulations governing disability compensation cases and compiled a multitude of helpful information in order to assist you. With my case it involved seeking a "total disability ratings for compensation based on un-employability" and/or a higher rating under Title 38 Part 4 Sec 4.16 and 4.18. This may sound like a foreign language to you right now but by the time you finish this book, you will have a full understanding on the matter.

I had one of the harder cases to settle. I contracted frostbite/chilblain to my feet while on guard duty in Germany in 1976. I had a hard nose little chubby Squad Sergeant I nicknamed butterball, who would not give me protective winter boots to wear while on duty. My feet eventually froze causing cold injuries to my feet. I was discharged honorably in 1979. Prior to my discharge I had gone and seen in-service medics and doctors at VA hospitals and clinics complaining about my feet but none of them did anything about it. You know the scenario; you come in and go out the same way. You might have been lucky enough to receive a couple of aspirin as I did. Anyway, after getting out and over the next thirty plus years my injuries became increasingly worst, so I went to VA hospitals and clinics to get help but mostly was seen by interns who poked and pried at my lower extremities and never came up with any solutions for treatment. Over time my legs and ankles swelled tremendously on a constant basis. I currently have pains in my heels that feel like walking on marbles and the rest of my feet feel like walking on bare bones. My legs ache with pain 24/7 on a daily basis. They feel tired and heavy, shooting pains running from the back of my feet and up through my legs and thighs. Eventually by the 90's as the medical field became more knowledgeable about cold injuries such as mine, I began to receive help from various private and VA medical specialist. I eventually was diagnosed with several conditions such as, nerve damage, circulatory insufficiencies, plantar fasciitis, chronic lymphedema and phlebitis, mental health issues from constantly being in pain, arthritis, tendonitis and a few other medical conditions. Till this day the symptoms still exist but have worsen to the point where I just could not work anymore by December 2007.

The process of requesting your compensation can be frustrating. When I first received my initial rating of 40% in 1998, I immediately appealed the Rating Boards decision. I kept my case open up until 2000. I had until May of 2000 to submit additional information that was requested of me. I waited until the last day allotted by the VA in order to submit this information with the assistance of an organization that I will not mention because I do not want to discourage anyone from using them just because I had a bad experience. The information was faxed to the proper VA department but I was told later by the VA Regional Office that they did not receive the paperwork by the one year deadline. By this time I was totally frustrated, broke and my family was suffering from the lack of money in the household, so I had to work through the pain for the next six to seven years off and on as my body would allow until there was nothing left in me mentally or physically. I'm quite sure a lot of you Vets can relate to this. I want to make sure that I can help you from not getting into this situation, hence the writing of this book.

What you need to understand is that when you put your case file together, you will need to gather copies of all medical records (private and VA) from your first day in service to the present and read them all before submitting anything. It does not benefit you to submit information that you have not read yet nor fully understand. Some documents may hurt your case so you want to make sure you are sending relevant information.

Another area you should be aware of is when you are with your doctor and you discuss information relating to your injuries, the majority of this conversation may not be placed in your medical records. I'd say 90% of compensation cases that are denied are because of the lack of clarity or missing information in your medical records. From this point on, you will learn not to let this happen. In later chapters I will discuss why but for right now I want you to get a glimpse at what documents we will be accumulating for your case. You will need to gather letters from doctors explaining your condition(s) fully, letters from employers, co-workers, friends and family members stating how your condition affects you when they see you. Are you agitated or grumpy? Do you have problems with being in crowds? All of this information will help your case. These documents will be submitted with your case file to the Rating Board. In later chapters you will learn how to package and send this information. All letters coming from, other than physicians should be notarized or at least add the following statement within "I certify that the information contained in this letter is true and correct to the best of my knowledge". This makes the letters more legitimate.

Per Title 38 3.200 Testimony certified or under oath.

a) All oral testimony presented by claimants and witnesses on their behalf before any rating or authorization body will be under oath or affirmation. (See §3.103(c).)
b) All written testimony submitted by the claimant or in his or her behalf for the purpose of establishing a claim for service connection will be certified or under oath or affirmation. This includes records, examination reports, and transcripts material to the issue received by the Department of Veterans Affairs at the instance of the claimant or in his or her behalf or requested by the Department of Veterans Affairs from State, county, municipal, recognized private institutions, and contract hospitals.

You will learn more about Title 38 in later sections of this book.

Important Note: Always make your doctor appointments. If you cannot make an appointment, make sure you cancel it giving a reason why and make sure it states so in the VA computer system. The individuals that you call to cancel your appointment will sometimes not input your reasoning for missed appointments. Be aware that the cancelation line and where you have appointments do not communicate well in certain VA clinics. You will think everything is alright until you get a copy of your records and they state you were a no show. We do not want this type of statement in your files. If you do not keep updated on your medical records, you will never know this was said, so stay current with your records. If you happen to notice such a statement in your records and you know that you canceled the appointment, immediately contact your doctors' office and have this corrected. Things of this nature can hurt your case. This may give the Rating Board the wrong impression of you.

You can also submit research reports. They are considered laymen evidence if it is obtained and presented by you. Take the time to learn the meaning of your medical condition(s). Have your doctor's break it down so that you understand exactly what your condition(s) is/are. If you still do not understand what they are saying the first time around, have the doctor break it down even further. Go online and look up the medical terms or go to the library and look through a medical dictionary. If you have vision problems most libraries have audio tapes for you to listen to. One thing I must warn you about. When you start looking up medical conditions, you may tend to think everything you see is what's wrong with you. Don't fall into this trap. It can affect your ability to put your case together because you feel everything you read is related to your medical problems. If you have concerns, write down the conditions and ask your doctor's for an opinion. (DON'T BE YOUR OWN DOCTOR. IT WILL NOT WORK WITH THE RATING BOARD)

Throughout this book I will use my case as examples. It's easier for you to comprehend how to write a statement if you can see a written example.

In the next chapter "Word Definitions" you will learn the lingo that is most commonly used by the VA Regional Offices and its Rating Boards and other verbiage used in the process. Do not skip any sections of this book. You must pick up this knowledge in order to understand fully the process. I can give you the tools but you must use them all.

It would be much easier for Vets to understand medical terminology if it would just be state in a way that everyone could understand. Now a day you have to have a standard and/or medical dictionary in your pocket to look up words.

The following departments of the VA and terms are most commonly used in correspondence that you may receive. I am not going to give you a five page list of items. My intent is only to define the most commonly used. We're not trying to acquire a degree here. However, it is imperative that you know about the various departments within the VA, and a small list of medical terms when describing your conditions in your letters sent to and received from the Rating Board. The following information was acquired online from the online Wikipedia dictionary, the VA main websites and its sub links and other medical websites mentioned throughout this text. All of this information is accessible to the public through the internet free of charge, so it can be verified.

Acute: In medicine, an **acute** disease with either or both of:
- A rapid onset;
- A short course (as opposed to a chronic course)

Example: One minute you're fine and the next minute you have an infection in your leg that may last for a short time.

Bilateral or Bilaterally: Having, or relating to, two sides. Bilateral is as opposed, for example, to unilateral (which means having, or relating to one side).
Example: You may hear a doctor say; swelling at the lower extremities bilaterally. In short, both of your legs or feet are swollen.
- Lower extremity bilaterally; both sides of your lower body
- Upper extremity bilaterally; both sides of the upper body

Board of Veterans' Appeals (BVA): Part of the Department of Veteran Affairs. It is located in Washington, DC. Members of the Board review appeals for VA benefits and make decisions on those appeals. If you have been denied benefits from your local VA Regional Office, you have the right to appeal to the BVA. You will have a choice of having a live appeals hearing with actual bodies there or a video conference. This is discussed further in later chapters. **Board of Veterans' Appeals, 810 Vermont Avenue, NW Washington, DC 20420**

Certification of Fully Developed Claim: This is a new form that the VA requires to be enclosed with your submission for compensation benefits. *"Expediting Fully Developed Claims:* On December 17, 2008, VA began a one-year pilot program at 10 regional offices to assess the feasibility and advisability of processing within 90 days after receipt fully developed compensation and pension claims. A *Certification of Fully Developed Claim* should accompany each claim submitted under this pilot program. For additional details, contact your SR and ask about the news release *VA Announces Pilot Program to Expedite "Fully Developed" Claims"*.

C-File: This is your entire military file, which includes personnel and medical records from your entrance into the Armed Services throughout your career and any personal and medical records that were accumulated after separation from the armed service for review in a disability or pension compensation case.

Chronic: A persistent and lasting disease or medical condition, or one that has developed slowly.
Example: You could have an infection in your arm and as soon as you get rid of it you get it again. It keeps coming back.

Code of Federal Regulations (CFR): The Code of Federal Regulations (CFR) is the codification (code) of the general and permanent rules published in the Federal Register by the executive departments and agencies of the Federal Government. It is divided into 50 titles that represent broad areas subject to Federal regulation. Each volume of the CFR is updated once each calendar year and is issued on a quarterly basis.

I call this the bible of all government benefits available to government employees, veterans and their families.

Compensation: Damages - legal term referring to the financial compensation recoverable by reason of another's breach of duty; the money paid or awarded to a plaintiff (you).

CUE: (Clear and Unmistakable Error). The decision is made by either the Department of Veterans Affairs Regional Office (VARO) or by the Board of Veterans' Appeals (BVA) or the Rating Board handling your present case. Minor inconsistencies do not constitute a CUE.

Example; you submitted doctor records that clearly state you have three injuries caused by a service connected injury and they explain why. When the Rating Officer (RO) makes a decision on your case they only give you compensation for one out of three injuries. This could be considered a CUE.

Decision Review Officer (DRO): DRO's offer a second review of your entire compensation file and can also hold a personal hearing on your case.

Example; If you are not satisfied with a decision that was made on your case you would file a Notice of Disagreement (NOD) and the VA would give you a choice of having a DRO review your case or go directly to through the BVA appeals process.

De Novo review/ Personal Hearing: Is a meeting between you, your SR (get a SR) if you have one and the DRO who can decide your appeal case. You have a right to ask for a DRO to review your file. In this case make sure you request a De Novo review if you are not going to be present. Basically, a DRO will review your case without you or your representative present. You can be present and show new material evidence if you want but that would be considered a Personal Hearing and not a De Novo.

Department of Veterans Affairs Regional Office (VARO): This is the main regional office for your local area. All business is initially conducted through this office.
Entitlement(s): It is a guarantee of access to benefits because of rights, or by agreement through law. It also refers, in a more casual sense to someone's belief that one is deserving of some particular reward or benefit.

Example; your case was settled and you have proven that your entitlements (the amount owed to you) should be worth $100,000 (that would be nice).

Etiology: The word is most commonly used in medical and philosophical theories, where it is used to refer to the study of why things occur, or even the reasons behind the way that things act.

Example; when a doctor writes a detailed report on your condition as to why and how and they look through your entire medical history to come up with a diagnosis this could be considered an etiology based report.

Extremity: The extremities in medical language are the uttermost parts of the body.

Example: The extremities are simply the hands, arms, feet and legs.

Laymen: To put something in layman's terms is to describe a complex or technical issue using words and terms that the average individual (someone without professional training in the subject area) can understand, so that they may comprehend the issue to some degree.

Example; if a doctor told me I have severe spinal stenosis at the L4-L5 level impinging on the thecal sac; my first words to him would be "WHAT". If they were to simply state that you have a disc that is pushing against the covering of your nerves in your back and it is located where you feel pain, this would be considered putting it in laymen terms.

Nexus: A connection or link. A causal connection or a connected series!

Example; when the VA asks you to show a nexus between let say, neuropathy and diabetes. What they are saying is show proof that your neuropathy is secondary, caused or aggravated by your diabetes or visa versa and how does having neuropathy make your diabetes worse.

Notice of Disagreement (NOD): If you disagree with your initial rating decision, you can write a statement to your local VA office saying that you disagree and that you want to appeal the decision or have a DRO review your case. The statement is called a Notice of Disagreement. There is no form for this. It is simply a hand or typed written by you to be submitted to the VA.

Rating Board: Rating Boards are located at your regional office in your area. Your initial claim folder is sent to this office for review by a Rating Officer (RO).

Rating Officer or Rating Specialist (RO) or (RS): This is the person that reviews your request for compensation. They make the first decision on your case.

Reasonable Doubt: In short, if you have one doctor who states in written form that you have certain ailments which are secondary, caused or aggravated by your reported service connected injury and they write a complete report explaining their findings and then you have a different doctor, possibly one the Rating Board sent you to, stating just the opposite, that none of your present conditions are related to your service in the Armed Forces and they explain their reasoning, the benefit of doubt will fall to the veterans' side if your current doctor(s) explained fully why your disabilities are secondary, caused or aggravated by a service connected injury.

Research Reports: Medical records that you copy from a medical website or from medical books that will be submitted as laymen evidence to support your case. These reports should show a nexus (a connection) between your disabilities.

Service Representative (SR): A person employed by the Veterans Service Organization (VSO) to assist you with your claim and other inquiries. **MAKE SURE YOU GET ONE**

Special Monthly Compensation (SMC): VA can pay an added compensation (paid in addition to the regular Disability Compensation) to a veteran who, as a result of military service, incurred the loss or loss of use of specific organs or extremities. Loss, or loss of use, is described as either an amputation or, having no effective remaining function of an extremity or organ

Statement of Case (SOC): SOC is a detailed explanation of evidence, laws and regulations used by the local VA office in deciding your claim. This correspondence is sent to you from the Rating Board explaining the reason for their decision on your case. You would receive this whether appealing a case or if it is a new case.

Title 38: One of 50 titles from the Code of Federal Regulations (CFR) book or found through their website that represent broad areas subjects to Federal regulation. You will learn more about this is later chapters.

VCAA Notice of Response: This form gives you the option of deciding your claim with the documents the VA has on hand or sending new supporting documents that you want the VA to review. Also, if there is any missing information needed by the Rating Board it would be requested of you in this letter. The letter gives you sixty additional days to submit additional documents. Of course I went with the additional sixty days.

VA Form 9: This form is sent to you along with the SOC. This is the last step relating to appealing a decision that was made on your case. Here you would be requesting that the **Board of Veterans' Appeals (BVA)** review your case. A sample copy is in the form section.

Veterans Service Center: Veterans Service Centers (VSC) are located in Albany, Bath, Canandaigua, Western New York, Syracuse and the Rochester Outpatient Clinic. These centers were designed to provide easy access and up to date information on Veterans health benefits. The Veterans Service Center can assist with beneficiary travel, patient funds program, decedent affairs, compensation and pension, and hospital services for overnight accommodations. Each facility has a Veterans Service Center Manager who handles local management of the Veterans Service Center. Veterans Service Center Managers: Handles local management of the Veterans Service Center.

James Arrington
Albany Veterans Service
Center Manager
Phone:
(518) 626-6722
Address:
James Arrington
VA Healthcare Network Upstate New York
113 Holland Avenue
Albany, NY 12208

James Jenkins
Bath Veterans Service
Center Manager
Phone:

(607) 664-4866
Fax: (607) 664-4915
Address:
James Jenkins
Bath VA Medical Center
76 Veterans Avenue
Bath, NY 14810

Deborah James

Canandaigua Veterans
Service Center Manager
Rochester Outpatient Clinic Veterans Service Center Manager
Phone: (585) 393-7347
Address:
Deborah James
Canandaigua VA Medical Center
400 Fort Hill Avenue
Canandaigua, NY 14424

Rebecca Keough

Syracuse Veterans Service
Center Manager
Phone:
(315) 425-4619
Fax: (315) 425-4344
Address:
Rebecca Keough
Syracuse VA Medical Center
800 Irving Avenue
Syracuse, NY 13210

Barbara Orlowski

Western New York Veterans
Service Center Manager
Phone:
(716) 862-6316
Address:
Barbara Orlowski
Buffalo VA Medical Center
3495 Bailey Avenue
Buffalo, NY 14215

Veterans Service Organization (VSO): They help Vets and are organizations such as, The American Legion, Disabled American Veterans, etc., as well as attorneys or agents recognized by the VA.

These are the major departments and terms we will be dealing with. If you have further questions about other medical terms, your medicine or medical condition, there are good

sources on the internet such as, MedicineNet
(http://www.medterms.com/script/main/hp.asp). Take a look at the website.

Assistance that may be available to you is not publicized to the point of seeing it on a 30 minute television programs or radio shows. You may see or hear brief information, but nothing to the extent of going through the entire process as I show you in this book.

When the VA begins to send you correspondence about your case, they mention where you can go to get additional information. A lot of Vets do not explore this option for reasons I cannot explain. Currently, the VA has a handbook available to you called "Federal Benefits for Veterans and Dependents". Simply go to your nearest VA center and request a copy. You may also call the toll free number at 1.800.827.1000 and request a copy or go online to http://www1.va.gov/opa/vadocs/current_benefits.asp and download a copy. Don't ignore references made in correspondences received from the VA or the above handbook telling you where you can find additional information. The more you educate yourself on how Rating Boards views information in your files you will be better prepared when you need to approach a physician requesting a descriptive medical report on your condition. There are actually set guidelines that ROs' must abide by, which I have placed in this reading for your review. In some correspondence that you will eventually receive from a Rating Board will quote some of these rules when explaining how they came to a particular conclusion in your case. I will show you how you can use and quote some of these same rules for your benefit in later chapters by showing you my letters that was sent to support my case. Again, educating yourself on the subject will greatly increase the chances for success.

The next chapter, Important Websites will show you where to go in order to obtain information related to your case. The beginning of this book may seem boring but it is important that you read all text in order to get a good grasp on the process. I am showing you everything that I did to get my case approved, so use it to your benefit. If you jump around from chapter to chapter you will miss something important. If I can save you from going through the frustrations that usually accompanies filing for compensation benefits, wouldn't you agree that it would be worth it? So use this book for what it is intended for "acquiring your disability or pension compensation benefits".

LET'S GET THROUGH THIS NEXT CHAPTER SO WE CAN INDULGE INTO THE FINER POINTS

Board of Veterans Appeals: http://www.index.va.gov/search/va/bva.html
- This site allows you to review past and present appeals referencing disability and pension compensation cases. I recommend reading as many of these cases as you can. You will gain valuable insight as to how the appeals process works. It will also let you see why some cases are turned down. Most of the time, it is because of the lack of medical evidence or clarity of the reports. Simply type in a condition such as cold injuries and it will show appeal cases relating to that subject.

Code of Federal Regulations (CFR) main page:
http://www.gpoaccess.gov/cfr/index.html
- Here you can research information contained in Title 38. Again, you will learn more about this in later chapters.

Compensation and Pension online application: http://vabenefits.vba.va.gov/vonapp/
- You can apply for your disability online.

MyHealtheVet: https://www.myhealth.va.gov/mhv-portal-web/anonymous.portal?_nfpb=true&_nfto=false&_pageLabel=mhvHome
- The Veterans Affairs has added a very informative website link to their home pages (My HealtheVet). This site allows you to order you medication online, access to medical health research and just a lot of good health news. Currently, the VA is making it possible for you to access and read some of your medical records. **Speak with your SR to learn how to request a DS login pass code.** Make sure you register at the MyHealtheVet site first so that you can access these features that are available to you. I cannot stress how important it is for you to register at this site. When it is available for you to review your records, you will not have to go to a veteran's center to get copies of certain medical records. You know how frustrating that can be if you've had to do it before. There is a form that can be printed out so that you can take it in person to the VA. Ask your SR for help.
- This website also has a few sections that I want you to visit but you have to register.

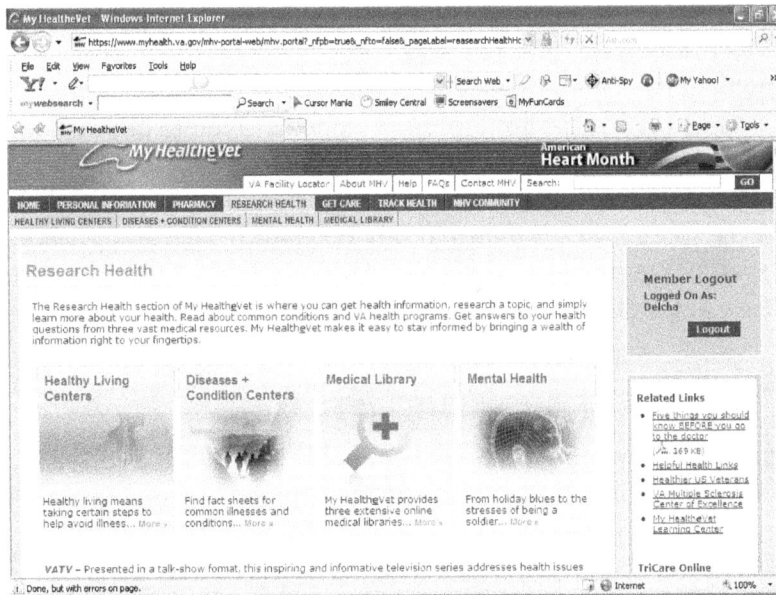

The Research Health section of MyHealtheVet is where you can obtain health information, research a topic and simply learn more about your health and/or medical problem. Read about common conditions and VA health programs. Get answers to your health questions from three vast medical resources. My HealtheVet makes it easy to stay informed by bringing a wealth of information right to your fingertips. Here you have four different categories that will be of interest to you, Healthy Living Centers, Diseases + Condition Centers, Mental Health and Medical Library. Out of the four, Diseases + Condition Centers and Medical Library are my favorites. Here you can find information on your disability. Medical Library will take you to MedlinePlus. When you receive medical literature from your VA primary doctor on your medical conditions, this is the most commonly used medical website. Other Veteran Medical Centers use MedlinePlus also.

The following additional sites can be used for you to download or print research documents referencing your medical condition. These reports will be considered laymen evidence that can be submitted with your application or appeal:

- The Merck Manuals http://www.merck.com/mmpe/index.html
  WebMD http://www.webmd.com/
  VascularWeb http://www.vascularweb.org/Pages/default.aspx

United States Court Of Appeals For Veterans Claims: http://www.uscourts.cavc.gov/

- The United States Court of Appeals for Veterans Claims is a national court of record, established under Article I of the Constitution of the United States. The Court has exclusive jurisdiction to provide judicial review of final decisions by the Board of Veterans' Appeals, an entity within the Department of Veterans Affairs.

The Court provides veterans an impartial judicial forum for review of administrative decisions by the Board of Veterans' Appeals that are adverse to the veteran-appellant's claim of entitlement to benefits for service-connected disabilities, survivor benefits and other benefits such as education payments and waiver of indebtedness. In furtherance of its mission, the Court also seeks to help ensure that all veterans have equal access to the Court and to promote public trust and confidence in the Court.

U.S. Department of Veterans Affairs (VARO): http://www.va.gov/

- This is the home page for the U.S. Department of Veterans Affairs. From this site you can find all information concerning services available to veterans. Get familiar with this site. This is your portal to obtaining valuable information to set up your disability compensation or pension case. You can also find Department of Veterans Affairs Regional Offices (VARO) in your state.

U.S. Government Printing Office (GPO) main page:
http://www.gpoaccess.gov/index.html

- The U.S. Government Printing Office disseminates official information from all three branches of the Federal Government

TITLE 38: Part 3_Adjudication Pensions, Bonuses, and Veteran's Relief

- I call this one "Bible Two" for information on disability compensation and pension for Veterans and Federal Employees. This section will also give you information helpful to your case. You can go to http://www.access.gpo.gov/nara/cfr/waisidx_08/38cfr3_08.html and review the entire section.

TITLE 38: Part 4_Schedule for Rating Disabilities Pension, Bonus, and Veterans Relief

- I call this the Bible for information on disability compensation and pension. Here is where you can find out exactly what the Rating Board looks for so far as, documentation when submitting your application for disability compensation or pension. You can go to http://www.access.gpo.gov/nara/cfr/waisidx_08/38cfr4_08.html and review the entire section.

Veterans Compensation Benefits Rate:
http://www.vba.va.gov/bln/21/rates/comp01.htm

- Here you can find out how much compensation (dollar amount) you could be eligible for.

USA.Gov: http://www.usa.gov/
- Government information site, jobs etc.

My website: http://delchapw.com/

In the next chapter "Things You May Not Have Known", we will go over information you may or may not have known about referencing compensation benefits

In the beginning of this section, I want to talk about some of the good stuff you've been waiting on. First let's talk about the **Code of Federal Regulations (CFR).** The CFR are important rules and regulations that effect how the Feds approve federal benefits in all classification under our government. The following three paragraphs give a short definition for the CFR as quoted directly from its print so as not to give incorrect information.

"The Code of Federal Regulations (CFR) is the codification (code) of the general and permanent rules published in the Federal Register by the executive departments and agencies of the Federal Government. It is divided into 50 titles that represent broad areas subject to Federal regulation. Each volume of the CFR is updated once each calendar year and is issued on a quarterly basis". (**Rules that the government puts out to enforce how benefits will be applied, rated and approved**)

"Each title is divided into chapters, which usually bear the name of the issuing agency. Each chapter is further subdivided into parts that cover specific regulatory areas. Large parts may be subdivided into subparts. All parts are organized in sections, and most citations in the CFR are provided at the section level. A list of agencies and where they appear in the CFR may be found in Appendix C of the U.S. Government Manual."

"The online CFR is a joint project authorized by the publisher, the National Archives and Records Administration's (NARA) Office of the Federal Register (OFR), and the Government Printing Office (GPO) to provide the public with enhanced access to Government information." "Documents are available in PDF and ASCII text formats. The Code of Federal Regulations is available on *GPO Access* from 1996 (partial) forward."

This seems to be a lot of jargon right, but it's not. You need to really get into reading or have someone read for you. You should know that the information I or anyone else gives you about federal benefits is correct. You can read the above text on the GPO's (U.S. Government Printing Office) website at http://www.gpoaccess.gov/cfr/about.html or just about any Public Library has a copy of the CFR in book form. The only problem about reviewing the book, libraries will not let you take it out. You have to read it there. There may be a sound version of the CFR but you will have to check with your local library or the Government Printing Office to see if they offer one. Now a day, most libraries have computers for your use. If you are not computer savvy, librarians will assist you. Just write down the website addresses you want to see from this book and give it to them. It's better to look at it on the internet and print out or download the specific pages you want to keep that relate to your case. The libraries usually charges 0.10¢ per copy for prints.

We will only be working with information shown in the following Parts of Title 38 under the CFR. Those are:

- TITLE 38: Part 3 Adjudication Pensions
  (http://www.access.gpo.gov/nara/cfr/waisidx_03/38cfr3_03.html)
- TITLE 38: Part 4 Schedule for Rating Disabilities Pension
  (http://www.access.gpo.gov/nara/cfr/waisidx_04/38cfr4_04.html)

Trying to search through the CFR can be confusing, that's why I'm giving you a direct link to the sections we will cover. Let's first start with Part 3 Adjudication Pensions. If you go online you will have the choice of viewing this title either as an Adobe or a Text file. I prefer the text version because it is more user friendly. What you are looking at defines rules that are applied in order to receive disability or pension compensation. There are other items discussed that you can review on your own, but we are going to stick with the ones referencing disability and pension compensation.

Let's go to Sec 3.2 Periods of War. This section sets forth the beginning and ending dates of each war period beginning with the Indian war. Example of other wars; World War I, World War II, Vietnam era, Persian Gulf War, etc. Sec 3.2 is basically letting you know what periods the VA will consider acceptable periods of war and peace time service for disability and pension compensation.

Next, open up Sec 3.3 Pension. By definition: A benefit payable monthly by the Department of Veterans Affairs because of non-service-connected disability or age and must have served 90 days or more to receive benefits plus the following:

- If you were injured during the 90 day period and VA medical records show this injury as services connected and is permanently and totally disabled from non-service connected disability not due to the veteran's own willful misconduct or vicious habits or by reason of having attained the age of 65 years or by reason of having become unemployable after age 65.

The above is quoted from Sec 3.3 and basically informs you of the requirements to establish eligibility for pension payments. The paperwork to receive such pension should be filled out in front of a SR or at least go over the form with a SR if you plan on submitting your documents on your own. This way, you can find out immediately the eligibility requirements. This section is really looking at your age, if you are totally disable or unemployable due to a non-service connected injury, if you presently have a pension from other sources or have you filled out the necessary paperwork to request pension compensation. It further speaks of your net worth making sure it is not over the applicable maximum annual pension rate specified in Sec. 3.23; which references:

- Veterans in need of aid and attendance.
- Veterans who are housebound.
- Two veterans married to one another; combined rates.

- Surviving spouse alone or with a child or children of the deceased veteran in custody of the surviving spouse.
- Surviving spouses in need of aid and attendance.
- Surviving spouses who are housebound.

Making sure you understand the above criteria is why you should have a SR on your side. Trying to complete the paperwork needed and trying to understand exactly what the VA is looking for can be confusing and frustrating. I cannot stress the importance of a SR **(GET ONE)**. If you're doing this on your own, at least set up an appointment to see a SR before you submit your file. It won't hurt to get a second opinion.

Now, let's go to Sec 3.4 Compensation. Here is where we get your beginning knowledge on what the Rating Board and/or Rating Officer (RO) looks at when reviewing your compensation case file. For our purposes, we will be indulging strictly with disability and pension compensation information.

When applying there are different types of compensation to look at:
- 0 to 90% disability rating
- 100% disability and pension compensation
- Total disability based on unemployability
- Additional compensation for spouse and child, to include step and foster children
- Dependent care for parents

"You must at least have a 30% or more rating to collect additional compensation for a spouse, child, and/or dependent parent(s).

I am generalizing a lot of the above information because I want you to get the bigger picture, which is, getting you prepared for your case submission. Make sure you inform the SR about your dependents if you want to get paid for them. They will need to know who you are taking care of as well as all of your children under 18 years of age. Once known, the SR will add them to your case if they are eligible. If you are like a lot of grandparents, it is not unusual for your grandkids to be living with you on a permanent bases. In order for you to receive additional compensation, educational and medical benefits for them, you will have to adopt them. Having simple custody of the kids is not acceptable to the VA.

The balance of Sec 3.4 speaks of additional money for aid of a housebound wife or child, survivor benefits, receiving additional monies for parents under your care etc. This is also a good reading point for you. God willing it won't happen soon, but if a veteran becomes deceased, you will want your spouse and/or children to know what benefits may be available to them. If you have a family trust, make sure your attorney is aware that you are a disabled veteran and show them Sec 3 especially if you have your VA checks going directly into your trust bank account. There may be something in there that may cause your attorney to modify your trust. For those of you, who do not have a Family Trust, seek the advice of a Trust Attorney. You might like what you hear. I know speaking about death is taboo but making sure there is a smooth transition for your spouse and family after a veterans demise can relieve a lot of stress on them. The last thing your family should have to worry about is finances. *This is just a thought to ponder.*

For my Philippino brothering, dating back to 1941 as a part of the Commonwealth Army of the Philippines or Philippine Scouts you could be eligible to receive benefits for compensation, dependency and indemnity compensation, and burial allowance from and after the dates and hours, respectively, when they were called into service of the Armed Forces of the United States by orders issued from time to time by the General Officer, U.S. Army, pursuant to the Military Order of the President of the United States dated July 26, 1941. Service as a guerrilla under the circumstances outlined in paragraph (d) of this section is also included.

These are quotes from Sec 3.

In today's army, American Philippino's serve as regular armed forces, so there is no special circumstances in order to receive compensation for disability or pension if you qualify. More information is available on the above under Sec 3.42.

Look through Title 38 Part 3 and write down the sections you feel pertains to your case. It makes it easier for you to reference back to this information when you need it. If you presently have a disability rating or even if you are putting a case together for the first time the information contained in Part 3 will benefit you greatly.

This concludes TITLE 38 Part 3. Now we will move onto TITLE 38: Part 4. This is the most important information we can access to assist you in preparing your file and to assist your doctors in writing etiology reports on your medical condition(s). You will learn about:

Keeping accurate copies of your medical records and keeping them up-to-dated.
- Whenever you see a private doctor you should always show them your VA medical records pertaining to your service connected condition(s). It might be easier for the doctor to review them if you have your records scanned and placed on a CD. To tell you the truth, doctors hate flipping through a large quantity of papers. Modern technology has spoiled all of us. The records will assist them in accurately diagnosing your medical condition(s) and enable them to write a very descriptive etiology report. If you have appointments with VA doctors, simply tell

them the dates of records that are associated with your service related condition(s) and they can pull it up on their system. I prefer to keep on hand a list of dates and places to give them so VA physicians can look through the reports. You will however have to take private doctor records with you to VA appointments for review. This is one of the reasons why you should review your medical records and write down dates, your medical condition(s) and the location of all records that relate to medical injuries that you feel are service related. You want to make sure that all of your doctors (private and VA) and the RO's knows where to look. In later chapters you will see the importance.

How medical records/reports can make or break your case.
- When you go and see your new or existing VA primary or private doctor for what you feel are service related injuries, you should always make sure that any diagnosis made by doctors are written down an placed in your medical file. I'll give you an example why. I went to a therapy session and I asked the therapist why my knees were hurting so much. He told me it was because of the way I changed my gait (the way you walk) to take some of the pressure off my feet. When I received a copy of the therapist notes (I always keep my medical records up-to-date) nothing about our conversation was entered. I asked the therapist why and he told me he did not think to do so and he did not know it was important, in which I expressed my concerns by telling him I'm not asking you to lie, just state your diagnoses and our conversation about my condition in my medical file. Since then everything that the therapist and I spoke of, especially when he made a diagnosis was placed in the medical file they kept on me. I did not curse the doctor out I simply spoke to him in a normal tone expressing my concerns. It has worked with every doctor that I have spoken to sense.

  Why is this important? If you're expressing to the Rating Board that your knee hurts because of the way you walk attempting to relief the pain from your feet and you are seeking additional disability compensation for that knee injury, you will need medical documentation showing your knee pain is secondary, caused or aggravated by your service connected injury(ies). If the information is not in the medical records, the Rating Board will dismiss your request or ask you to supply additional information for that disability because they could not find any evidence. This will lead to (1) dismissing the claim or (2) more downtime in deciding your case. Option (2) could take up to an additional six months to get a response from the Rating Board. It is important to remember the smallest minute missing detail could hurt or delay your case and we do not want that.

Have your doctor(s) order as many test as necessary to define your disability.
- Vets have it easier than non-vets when it comes to receiving free or paying for

medical treatment. You can find the healthcare schedule at http://www4.va.gov/healtheligibility/Library/AnnualThresholds.asp, which will show you eligibility requirements in order to utilize VA health care facilities. We as Vets receive treatment much cheaper or in some cases free then nonveterans. Since I am considered 100% unemployable, I fall under a category which allows me free medical treatment from any VA or Federal medical facility and my medication is free. I additionally receive free private hospital treatment for emergencies and fee base appointments (when the VA authorizes you treatment at a private facility). If you become eligible for such private services, stay on top of payments to be made to them by the VA. If the VA does not pay the bill within a certain time limit, the private hospital will bill you. If you do not take care of the bill, they will put a delinquent debt on your credit report. You have a two year time limit to notify the VA of old medical bills coming from private fee base medical facilities. Once this time limit has expired, you will be responsible for payment.

As mentioned previously, once you are rated 50% or higher, your medication will be free. Let your primary doctor take as many test as it takes to diagnose your medical condition. You'll need these reports. Also make sure that any medication that is given to you for a service related injury is clearly marked "service connected" in your file. If it is not, you will be charged co-pays if your service rating is less than 50%.

When it comes to your joints, many doctors only take x-rays. This does not always show a problem. As an example; I had x-rays of my feet and it only showed that I had soft tissue edema and arthritic changes in my feet. I knew there was something else wrong so I requested a MRI, which revealed multiple problems such as, hemorrhaging in one of my heels and water in my joints. X-rays may not give a clear picture of your injuries. Another example; I hurt my back in the early 90's. The company I worked for sent me to a Ready Care Facility (an industrial medical clinic contracted with many companies). The only thing this doctor would do is shoot me up with steroids and get x-rays. I told him there had to be something else wrong. He ignored what I was saying and sent me to therapy. I refused therapy around the second week into it because of constant pain. I eventually changed doctors and went to Stanford Medical Center in Northern California. Once under their care I was sent for a MRI on my back, where it was found that I had a severe herniated disc and that I should not have been in any physical therapy. I was actually hurting my condition.

Point being, you should ask your doctor about other test that can be performed to give a clearer picture of your condition. Ask could a CT or MRI scan, Ultra

Sound or Dobbler test show a more define picture of your injuries. Sometimes you have to become a little more aggressive but nice.

Learning what set of rules the Rating Board abides by.

- Under the CFR, the RO should review your medical records tracing back through your entire medical history relating to your service injury in order to get a clear understanding of your condition. This particular statement refers to individuals seeking a higher rating, an appeal and in some cases a new submission. In a lot of medical cases, an injury can take years to progress to a point of severe pain on a constant basis and might need to be researched a little deeper by the RO. This is another reason why you should write down dates, location and medical conditions so the RO can go straight to those files.

Now let us get into Part 4. The following sections will explain what the RO looks for when examining your case file. All RO's abide by the same guidelines found in Title 38 Part 4. I have arranged the sections in order of importance. First you will see paragraphs that I obtained directly from the actual CFR website so as not to give you improper information, followed by an example. This way when you speak with your SR you can state your feelings as well as understand what they might say referencing the CFR. It is a lot easier to work with your SR if you have some general knowledge on the subject. The way you perceive the meaning of a section may not necessarily be right.

TITLE 38: Part 4.

Sec. 4.1 Essentials of evaluative rating.

This section is primarily a guide in the evaluation of disability resulting from all types of diseases and injuries encountered as a result of military service. The percentage ratings represent as far as can practically be determined the average impairment in earning capacity resulting from such diseases and injuries and their residual conditions in civil occupations. Generally, the degrees of disability specified are considered adequate to compensate for considerable loss of working time from exacerbations or illnesses proportionate to the severity of the several grades of disability. For the application of this schedule, <u>accurate and fully descriptive medical examinations are required, with emphasis upon the limitation of activity imposed by the disabling condition</u>. Over a period of many years, a veteran's disability claim may require re-ratings in accordance with changes in laws, medical knowledge and his or her physical or mental condition. <u>It is thus essential, both in the examination and in the evaluation of disability, that each disability be viewed in relation to its history</u>".

- This is a general introduction to Sec. 4. Basically, it's letting you see out of the eyes of a RO and how they should review your entire case file. Make note of the underlined areas. These are little settles rules that may be overlooked by you and the RO. If your medical records are not clear the RO cannot make a decisive decision. When you submit your new, re-rating or appeals request, you want to make sure that the RO has accurate information. RO's follow their guidelines to the letter. They do however make mistakes on occasion but if your file is package correctly with the correct information the first time around there should not be much of a clarity problem. By giving location and dates so that RO's can search for specific medical records/conditions that speak of your injury will help your case tremendously. I can tell you from experience, the RO will not just look through a two inch file. They have many files that hit their desk and they do not have time and probably the patients to search through every report, but if you give dates and locations based on your VA medical records they can go directly to those reports and if they show clear cut evidence of your service connection condition(s) you will be rated appropriately. Also you protect yourself just in case you do get a RO who states that certain files or documents were not enclosed when you know for sure they were submitted. If this does happen you are suppose to receive a letter from the Rating Board letting you know that information is missing and you will have 30 days from the date of the correspondence to get such evidence back to them. At least this way you are alerted that a problem exist, which can be corrected easily. Put yourself in their shoes. They receive hundreds of case files per day. It's easy for something to slip between the cracks with such a repetitive job.

Do not send records that do not pertain to your injury or case. This causes unwarranted down time for your decision because the RO is reviewing an injury that has nothing to do with your case. Again, this is where having a SR on your side is a good thing. They are aware of such mistakes Vets make. Simply go through your records first, find the reports that are linked to your service related injury and only submit that information.

The following is a sample of how to write down important dates:

DATE: mm/dd/yyyy	LOCATION OF RECORDS AND MEDICAL CONDITION
01/01/1954	San Francisco, CA VA Med Center – Cellulites of the lower extremities
04/25/1962	Monterey, CA VA Med Center – Frostbite of left foot

06/06/1964	Sacramento, CA – Dr. John Jones (private doctor) Diabetes, Lower extremity lymphedema, cellulites

Believe me the RO will appreciate your thoroughness. I have formatted a word document in which you can use. You can download it from my website at http://delchapw.com/.

As you can see the above form shows dates and locations along with a brief description of medical conditions.
My trials and errors will be your success.

Sec. 4.2 Interpretation of examination reports.

Different examiners, at different times, will not describe the same disability in the same language. Features of the disability which must have persisted unchanged may be overlooked or a change for the better or worse may not be accurately appreciated or described. It is the responsibility of the rating specialist to interpret reports of examination in the light of the whole recorded history, reconciling the various reports into a consistent picture so that the current rating may accurately reflect the elements of disability present. Each disability must be considered from the point of view of the veteran working or seeking work. If a diagnosis is not supported by the findings on the examination report or if the report does not contain sufficient detail, it is incumbent upon the Rating Board to return the report as inadequate for evaluation purposes.

- This section is a nice thought but it is not always done. Again, the RO has many case files of other veterans to review beyond yours and may overlook important information that you have submitted. This is not giving them an excuse but letting you know the reality of how thing might be. On the other hand, if the information is not clear in your records, the RO cannot be held responsible for missing it and/or dismissing your claim. As an example; if the Rating Board sets up an examination and the examiner neglected to explain or make a judgment on certain conditions, the RO can request the examiner to redo or clarify their findings. It's totally up to the reviewing RO, so it is very important that you make sure your reports are clear prior to submission. Look at it this way, if you feel the doctors has explained your condition(s) fully and the information clearly states that your condition is service connected, then the RO should feel the same based off of medical evidence. The report must clearly state why the doctor feels a condition is service related. You can review one of my VA and private doctor letters on my website.

Sec. 4.3 Resolution of reasonable doubt.

Title 38 Part 3 Sec 3.102: It is the defined and consistently applied policy of the

Department of Veterans Affairs to administer the law under a broad interpretation, consistent, however, with the facts shown in every case. When, after careful consideration of all procurable and assembled data, a reasonable doubt arises regarding service origin, the degree of disability, or any other point, such doubt will be resolved in favor of the claimant. <u>By reasonable doubt is meant one which exists because of an approximate balance of positive and negative evidence which does not satisfactorily prove or disprove the claim.</u> It is a substantial doubt and one within the range of probability as distinguished from pure speculation or remote possibility. It is not a means of reconciling actual conflict or a contradiction in the evidence. Mere suspicion or doubt as to the truth of any statements submitted, as distinguished from impeachment or contradiction by evidence or known facts, is not justifiable basis for denying the application of the reasonable doubt doctrine if the entire, complete record otherwise warrants invoking this doctrine. The reasonable doubt doctrine is also applicable even in the absence of official records, particularly if the basic incident allegedly arose under combat or similarly strenuous conditions, and is consistent with the probable results of such known hardships.

- This is definitely true. The laws governing disability does give the veteran the reasonable doubt factor if the evidence toward good versus bad are evenly weighed. Example; if one doctor states you have diabetes and it was secondary, caused or aggravated by a condition related to your service in the Armed Forces and he/she fully explains why he/she thinks so and another doctor states that the diabetes is not service related and also explains their reasons and the weight of the two reports are evenly balanced, the RO should rule in favor of the veteran. This ruling is called "reasonable doubt".

Sec. 4.6 Evaluation of evidence.

The element of the weight to be accorded the character of the veteran's service is but one factor entering into the considerations of the Rating Boards in arriving at determinations of the evaluation of disability. Every element in any way affecting the probative value to be assigned to the evidence in each individual claim must be thoroughly and conscientiously studied by each member of the Rating Board in the light of the established policies of the Department of Veterans Affairs to the end that decisions will be equitable and just as contemplated by the requirements of the law.

- As stated, all evidence should be weighed evenly. They are giving the Rating Board a little lead way when rating you based on their policies. Let's say your rating falls in between two rating criteria's like diabetes for example. Per Sec. 4.119, Schedule of ratings endocrine system Sub Sec 7913, for a 40% rating you must fall under the following; "requiring insulin, restricted diet, and regulation of activities" and for a 20% rating the requirements are, "requiring insulin and restricted diet, or; oral hypoglycemic agent and restricted diet". The deference in getting the higher of the two ratings is the addition of one medical condition "regulation of activities". Let's go further and say, over a five year period you were restricted to regulating your activities. You're not to do any stressful activities like exercise, picking up things etc. To some RO's this might not be enough to give you a higher rating but to others it may. This is what I mean by the Rating Board having a little lead way. The decision could go either way. It's up to you to send the necessary medical evidence proving your case. If the RO decides against you the first time around this does not necessarily mean they are correct.

Sec. 4.7 Higher of two evaluations

Where there is a question as to which of two evaluations shall be applied, the higher evaluation will be assigned if the disability picture more nearly approximates the criteria required for that rating. Otherwise, the lower rating will be assigned.

- In some cases the RO has a decision to make when a disability is in between ratings. In my case the RO reviewed my diagnosis of Mood Disorder. Some of the information classified me as 30%. On the other hand my condition was seen to be over the 30% classification and more closely resembled a 50% classification. This led the RO to assign a 50% rating to my case. This reflects back to me stating that you should make sure your doctor reports a clear as to your condition.

Sec. 4.9 Congenital or developmental defects.

Mere congenital or developmental defects, absent, displaced or supernumerary parts, refractive error of the eye, personality disorder and mental deficiency are not diseases or injuries in the meaning of applicable legislation for disability compensation purposes.

- This is a list of medical problems that is felt to be non-compensating injuries just on their own. Again, there must be clear cut evidence that the above disorders are caused or aggravate by a service related injury. Example; you are claiming that you have a mental disorder, so you put that on your list of disabilities secondary, caused or aggravated by a service related medical problem. In your mental health record (if you have one) it states you are under stress but fails to state it is secondary, caused or aggravated by your service connected ailments. This would not be considered a service related disability because there is no evidence in your medical file showing the connection. On the other hand, if you are seen by the mental health clinic once or twice per month because you have been stressed out or depressed due to your medical condition and you are having sleepless nights because of pain that you are claiming to be service connected etc., now you have something to go on. Do you see the difference? Having a metal health condition based on an injury you believe to be service connected, instead of being stressed out for other non-service related injuries. There are major differences. If you are claiming an injury, that problem must be stated in your medical records and it must be connected to the medical injury you are claiming service connection for. You can see a copy of my decision on my website.

I want to stop right here for a moment. There are two terms that I want you to be aware of that I used above (*secondary, caused or aggravated*). These terms if not used properly can affect your decision. When describing your injury to the Rating Board, make sure to use the right verbiage. If you have a non-service connected injury and it is written in your medical records that it has become worse because of your service connected injury, you would use the terms aggravate or aggravating. If on the other hand you have a services connected injury like diabetes and you begin to have other medical problems like going blind and your medical records state something to the effect that the current eye problems are caused by the veterans service connected diabetes, then you would use the term caused. It may seem like it is not that important but when the RO reviews your request and the wrong terminology is used, it can hurt your case tremendously. Having discussed this with a SR would eliminate this discrepancy.

Sec. 4.10 Functional impairment.

The basis of disability evaluations is the ability of the body as a whole, or of the psyche, or of a system or organ of the body to function under the ordinary conditions of daily life including employment. Whether the upper or lower extremities, the back or abdominal wall, the eyes or ears, or the cardiovascular, digestive, or other system, or psyche are affected, evaluations are based upon lack of usefulness, of these parts or systems, especially in self-support. This imposes upon the medical examiner the responsibility of furnishing, in addition to the etiological, anatomical, pathological, laboratory and prognostic data required for ordinary medical classification, full description of the effects of disability upon the person's ordinary activity. In this connection, it will be remembered that a person may be too disabled to engage in employment although he or she is up and about and fairly comfortable at home or upon limited activity.

- This goes back to what I stated earlier about making sure your doctors explains to the fullest extent your injuries. You're not asking them to give up their first born. You are simply asking the physician to evaluate you based on your injury. Let them know that you are submitting documents to the Rating Board and that you need a clear explanatory evaluation. Show your doctors these sections we are going over now. Just go online and copy and paste these sections and print them out. Some physicians may or may not look at it, but you must explain to them the importance. Most VA doctors, accept those who strictly perform compensation exams, are not aware of what Rating Boards are looking for. Again, you're not asking them to lie about your condition you simply need to have a clear explanation on your condition and how it affects your bodily system, your daily activities or ability to work and to enter their conclusion in your medical records as to how it is connected to your service related injuries.

Sec. 4.13 Effect of change of diagnosis.

The repercussion upon a current rating of service connection when change is made of a previously assigned diagnosis or etiology must be kept in mind. The aim should be the reconciliation and continuance of the diagnosis or etiology upon which service connection for the disability had been granted. The relevant principle enunciated in Sec. 4.125, entitled ``Diagnosis of mental disorders,'' should have careful attention in this connection. When any change in evaluation is to be made, the rating agency should assure itself that there has been an actual change in the conditions, for better or worse, and not merely a difference in thoroughness of the examination or in use of descriptive terms. This will not, of course, preclude the correction of erroneous ratings, nor will it preclude assignment of a rating in conformity with Sec. 4.7.

- This is pretty clear cut. When you are asking for a higher rating, the RO will make sure there has been a change in your condition. Your existing disability has to have changed for the worst or you feel the last rating missed something and you disagree with the decision. In both cases, you will have to submit new and material evidence (medical records or doctor statements that the Rating Board has not seen before) unless you feel there was an error, which could be considered a CUE (Clear and Unmistakable Error). In this case either the Department of Veterans Affairs Regional Office (VARO) or the Board of Veterans' Appeals (BVA) will make a decision as to the validity (if your claim has some weight to it) of your claim. CUE's are very hard to prove so get help applying for this.

  As an example; there was a case, which had a decision dated 05/06/08. In the decision, there was a clear CUE. The case can be viewed in its entirety at http://www.va.gov/vetapp08/files2/0814960.txt. Basically, the case was centered on the RO rating the veterans' disability as a single injury when in fact at the time the file was reviewed by the RO medical records clearly showed the veteran had multiple injuries that should have been rated. This case was considered a CUE and the veterans' rating was corrected. If you have a case similar to this one, you should file for CUE. Check with an SR to see how far back you can claim a CUE. Minor inconsistencies do not constitute a CUE.

Sec. 4.15 100% Total disability ratings.

The ability to overcome the handicap of disability varies widely among individuals. The rating, however, is based primarily upon the average impairment in earning capacity, that is, upon the economic or industrial handicap which must be overcome and not from individual success in overcoming it. However, full consideration must be given to unusual physical or mental effects in individual cases, to peculiar effects of occupational activities, to defects in physical or mental endowment preventing the usual amount of success in overcoming the handicap of disability and to the effect of combinations of disability. Total disability will be considered to exist when there is present any impairment of mind or body which is sufficient to render it impossible for the average person to follow a substantially gainful occupation; Provided that permanent total disability shall be taken to exist when the impairment is reasonably certain to continue throughout the life of the disabled person. The following will be considered to be permanent total disability: the permanent loss of the use of both hands, or of both feet, or of one hand and one foot, or of the sight of both eyes, or becoming permanently helpless or permanently bedridden. Other total disability ratings are scheduled in the various bodily systems of this schedule.

- This is a tough and a confusing one. Beyond your medical condition, the Rating Board will look strongly at your work history, training, schooling and what your doctors state your conditions are and how they affect your ability to work. Rating for total disability is definitely done on a case by case basis. A lot of veterans receiving total disability ratings usually are amputees, blind individuals or have no use of certain limbs as if they had been amputated. Again, as stated earlier you should sign up with a SR or attorney. Be advised, that an attorney is going to want a percentage of your compensation, whereas a SR can perform the same duties for free and in most cases have more experience when dealing with the Rating Board. SR's have attended a huge number of appeal cases. This gives them an advantage as to what information is needed and how to structure a case for submission. They can also decipher if you should request 100% disability or total disability based on unemployability as described below. To be truthful, it is easier to receive unemployability disability then 100% disabled. You receive the same monetary dollar amounts and services.

Sec. 4.16 Total disability ratings for compensation based on unemployability of the individual.

Total disability ratings for compensation may be assigned, where the scheduler rating is less than total, when the disabled person is, in the judgment of the rating agency, unable to secure or follow a substantially gainful occupation as a result of service-connected disabilities: Provided That, if there is only one such disability, this disability shall be ratable at 60 percent or more, and that, if there are two or more disabilities, there shall be at least one disability ratable at 40 percent or more, and sufficient additional disability to bring the combined rating to 70 percent or more. For the above purpose of one 60 percent disability, or one 40 percent disability in combination, the following will be considered as one disability: (1) Disabilities of one or both upper extremities, or of one or both lower extremities, including the bilateral factor, if applicable, (2) disabilities resulting from common etiology or a single accident, (3) disabilities affecting a single body system, e.g. orthopedic, digestive, respiratory, cardiovascular-renal, neuropsychiatric, (4) multiple injuries incurred in action, or (5) multiple disabilities incurred as a prisoner of war. It is provided further that the existence or degree of non-service connected disabilities or previous unemployability status will be disregarded where the percentages referred to in this paragraph for the service-connected disability or disabilities are met and in the judgment of the rating agency such service-connected disabilities render the veteran unemployable. Marginal employment shall not be considered substantially gainful employment. For purposes of this section, marginal employment generally shall be deemed to exist when a veteran's earned annual income does not exceed the amount established by the U.S. Department of Commerce, Bureau of the Census, as the poverty threshold for one person. Marginal employment may also be held to exist, on a facts found basis (includes but is not limited to employment in a protected environment such as a family business or sheltered workshop), when earned annual income exceeds the poverty threshold. Consideration shall be given in all claims to the nature of the employment and the reason for termination. (Authority: 38 U.S.C. 501) (b) It is the established policy of the Department of Veterans Affairs that all veterans who are unable to secure and follow a substantially gainful occupation by reason of service-connected disabilities shall be rated totally disabled. Therefore, Rating Boards should submit to the Director, Compensation and Pension Service, for extra-scheduler consideration all cases of veterans who are unemployable by reason of service-connected disabilities, but who fail to meet the percentage standards set forth in paragraph (a) of this section. The Rating Board will include a full statement as to the veteran's service connected disabilities, employment history, educational and vocational attainment and all other factors having a bearing on the issue.

- Similar to total disability rating with the acceptation of not having a total percentage rating of 100% as defined under Sec. 4.15, you must have a minimum percentage rating to qualify. To clear this requirements up a bit, you must have at least one disability that is currently rated at 60% or if you have two disabilities totaling 70% in order for you to be qualified to receive an unemployability rating. The catch all to this statement is when you are requesting disability compensation for the first time or requesting a higher rating, you can accumulate the eligible minimum percentage rating while your case is being reviewed. In other words, a RO can first rate your disabilities giving each a percentage rating and then combine them so that you meet the eligibility percentage. From there they will evaluate your case to see if you are unemployable.

The key word in the section is unemployable. As an example, if you're trying to hold down jobs and you keep getting laid off because you take too much time off because of your service disabilities interfering with work this could be considered one form of unemployability. You must have medical record that shows disabilities that stop you from working. This reverts back to my earlier statement, have your doctors explain your disability in detail and get letters from past employers and co-workers etc. It's one of the keys to a successful case!

Sec. 4.17 Total disability ratings for pension based on unemployability and age of the individual.

All veterans who are basically eligible and who are unable to secure and follow a substantially gainful occupation by reason of disabilities which are likely to be permanent shall be rated as permanently and totally disabled. For the purpose of pension, the permanence of the percentage requirements of Sec. 4.16 is a requisite. When the percentage requirements are met, and the disabilities involved are of a permanent nature, a rating of permanent and total disability will be assigned if the veteran is found to be unable to secure and follow substantially gainful employment by reason of such disability. Prior employment or unemployment status is immaterial if in the judgment of the Rating Board the veteran's disabilities render him or her unemployable. In making such determinations, the following guidelines will be used: (a) Marginal employment, for example, as a self-employed farmer or other person, while employed in his or her own business, or at odd jobs or while employed at less than half the usual remuneration will not be considered incompatible with a determination of unemployability, if the restriction, as to securing or retaining better employment, is due to disability.(b) Claims of all veterans who fail to meet the percentage standards but who meet the basic entitlement criteria and are unemployable, will be referred by the Rating Board to the Veterans Service Center Manager under Sec. 3.321(b)(2) of this chapter.

- Pretty much the same as unemployable Sec 4.16. The same rules apply with the exception, this is for pension cases and there is a minimum age requirement of 65.

Sec. 4.18 Unemployability.

A veteran may be considered as unemployable upon termination of employment which was provided on account of disability or in which special consideration was given on account of the same, when it is satisfactorily shown that he or she is unable to secure further employment. With amputations, sequelae of fractures and other residuals of traumatism shown to be of static character, a showing of continuous unemployability from date of incurrence, or the date the condition reached the stabilized level, is a general requirement in order to establish the fact that present unemployability is the result of the disability. However, consideration is to be given to the circumstances of employment in individual claims, and, if the employment was only occasional, intermittent, tryout or unsuccessful, or eventually terminated on account of the disability, present unemployability may be attributed to the static disability. Where unemployability for pension previously has been established on the basis of combined service connected and non-service-connected disabilities and the service connected disability or disabilities have increased in severity, Sec. 4.16 is for consideration.

- Continuation from Sec 4.17.

Sec. 4.19 Age in service-connected claims.

Age may not be considered as a factor in evaluating service connected disability; and unemployability, in service-connected claims, associated with advancing age or inter current disability, may not be used as a basis for a total disability rating. Age, as such, is a factor only in evaluations of disability not resulting from service, i.e., for the purposes of pension.

- Unlike Social Security where age does play apart, when determining disability cases, the VA does not use the age factor when deciding your disability, so do not harp on your age when structuring your case.

Sec. 4.20 Analogous ratings (a condition that is not listed for rating purposes)

When an unlisted condition is encountered it will be permissible to rate under a closely related disease or injury in which not only the functions affected, but the anatomical localization and symptomatology are closely analogous. Conjectural analogies will be avoided, as will the use of analogous ratings for conditions of doubtful diagnosis, or for those not fully supported by clinical and laboratory findings. Nor will ratings assigned to organic diseases and injuries be assigned by analogy to conditions of functional origin.

- In some circumstances, there will be conditions that you have that are not listed under a rating code. The RO will find the closes matching medical condition and make a determination based on the description of that condition and supporting facts within your case file.

Sec. 4.22 Rating of disabilities aggravated by active service.

In cases involving aggravation by active service, the rating will reflect only the degree of disability over and above the degree existing at the time of entrance into the active service, whether the particular condition was noted at the time of entrance into the active service, or it is determined upon the evidence of record to have existed at that time. It is necessary therefore, in all cases of this character to deduct from the present degree of disability the degree, if ascertainable, of the disability existing at the time of entrance into active service, in terms of the rating schedule, except that if the disability is total (100 percent) no deduction will be made. The resulting difference will be recorded on the rating sheet. If the degree of disability at the time of entrance into the service is not ascertainable in terms of the schedule, no deduction will be made.

- What this is saying is if you had a condition let's say, when you first entered the service and at that time the injury would have been rated at a 10% rating. When you are discharged and you apply for disability compensation for that injury that was aggravated by your time in service and when the RO makes their decision as to the percentage of your disability after discharge, they will deduct the 10% from your total rating unless it is seen that you are 100% disabled. The VA is currently attempting to standardize a system where prior to a Vet being released from service with a condition, they can have their claims approved before being discharged. This is a good thing. Though you may not see or hear about changes being made in the system, the VA is making settle changes to help Vets.

Sec. 4.23 Attitude of rating officers.

It is to be remembered that the majority of applicants are disabled persons who are seeking benefits of law to which they believe themselves entitled. In the exercise of his or her functions, rating officers must not allow their personal feelings to intrude; an antagonistic, critical, or even abusive attitude on the part of a claimant should not in any instance influence the officers in the handling of the case. Fairness and courtesy must at all times be shown to applicants by all employees whose duties bring them in contact, directly or indirectly, with the Department's claimants.

- In short, the RO is trained not to let personal feeling guide them in their decision.

Sec. 4.26 Bilateral factor.

When a partial disability results from disease or injury of both arms, or of both legs, or of paired skeletal muscles, the ratings for the disabilities of the right and left sides will be combined as usual, and 10 percent of this value will be added (i.e., not combined) before proceeding with further combinations, or converting to degree of disability. The bilateral factor will be applied to such bilateral disabilities before other combinations are carried out and the rating for such disabilities including the bilateral factor in this section will be treated as 1 disability for the purpose of arranging in order of severity and for all further combinations. For example, with disabilities evaluated at 60 percent, 20 percent, 10 percent and 10 percent (the two 10's representing bilateral disabilities), the order of severity would be 60, 21 and 20. The 60 and 21 combine to 68 percent and the 68 and 20 to 74 percent, converted to 70 percent as the final degree of disability. (a) The use of the terms ``arms'' and ``legs'' is not intended to distinguish between the arm, forearm and hand, or the thigh, leg, and foot, but relates to the upper extremities and lower extremities as a whole. Thus with a compensable disability of the right thigh, for example, amputation, and one of the left foot, for example, pes planus, the bilateral factor applies, and similarly whenever there are compensable disabilities affecting use of paired extremities regardless of location or specified type of impairment. (b) The correct procedure when applying the bilateral factor to disabilities affecting both upper extremities and both lower extremities is to combine the ratings of the disabilities affecting the 4 extremities in the order of their individual severity and apply the bilateral factor by adding, not combining, 10 percent of the combined value thus attained. (c) The bilateral factor is not applicable unless there is partial disability of compensable degree in each of 2 paired extremities, or paired skeletal muscles.

- This may be a little confusing. Take a look at the rating table below and I will walk you through the above example:

Table I--Combined Ratings Table [10 combined with 10 is 19]

	10	20	30	40	50	60	70	80	90
19	27	35	43	51	60	68	76	84	92
20	28	36	44	52	60	68	76	84	92
21	29	37	45	53	61	68	76	84	92
22	30	38	45	53	61	69	77	84	92
23	31	38	46	54	62	69	77	85	92
24	32	39	47	54	62	70	77	85	92
25	33	40	48	55	63	70	78	85	93
26	33	41	48	56	63	70	78	85	93
27	34	42	49	56	64	71	78	85	93
28	35	42	50	57	64	71	78	86	93
29	36	43	50	57	65	72	79	86	93
30	37	44	51	58	65	72	79	86	93
31	38	45	52	59	66	72	79	86	93
32	39	46	52	59	66	73	80	86	93
33	40	46	53	60	67	73	80	87	93
34	41	47	54	60	67	74	80	87	93
35	42	48	55	61	68	74	81	87	94
36	42	49	55	62	68	74	81	87	94
37	43	50	56	62	69	75	81	87	94
38	44	50	57	63	69	75	81	88	94
39	45	51	57	63	70	76	82	88	94
40	46	52	58	64	70	76	82	88	94
41	47	53	59	65	71	76	82	88	94
42	48	54	59	65	71	77	83	88	94
43	49	54	60	66	72	77	83	89	94
44	50	55	61	66	72	78	83	89	94
45	51	56	62	67	73	78	84	89	95
46	51	57	62	68	73	78	84	89	95
47	52	58	63	68	74	79	84	89	95
48	53	58	64	69	74	79	84	90	95
49	54	59	64	69	75	80	85	90	95
50	55	60	65	70	75	80	85	90	95
51	56	61	66	71	76	80	85	90	95
52	57	62	66	71	76	81	86	90	95
53	58	62	67	72	77	81	86	91	95
54	59	63	68	72	77	82	86	91	95
55	60	64	69	73	78	82	87	91	96
56	60	65	69	74	78	82	87	91	96
57	61	66	70	74	79	83	87	91	96
58	62	66	71	75	79	83	87	92	96

35

```
59........................................ 63 67 71 75 80 84 88 92 96
60........................................ 64 68 72 76 80 84 88 92 96
61........................................ 65 69 73 77 81 84 88 92 96
62........................................ 66 70 73 77 81 85 89 92 96
63........................................ 67 70 74 78 82 85 89 93 96
64........................................ 68 71 75 78 82 86 89 93 96
65........................................ 69 72 76 79 83 86 90 93 97
66........................................ 69 73 76 80 83 86 90 93 97
67........................................ 70 74 77 80 84 87 90 93 97
68........................................ 71 74 78 81 84 87 90 94 97
69........................................ 72 75 78 81 85 88 91 94 97
70........................................ 73 76 79 82 85 88 91 94 97
-------------------------------------------------------------------
```

Above we first look to the left. This is the first rating at 60. We then find 21 on the horizontal line at the top (rounded it becomes 20). We follow it down to 60 on the left vertical column and we come up with 68 at the meeting point. We then go back to the left vertical column and look for 68. Again, we look for the 20 on the horizontal line at the top. We follow it down to 68 and we come up with 74% total rating. Do not get too involved with the rating tables. The Rating Board handles this. I just wanted to let you see how it works and how to read the chart. If you ever think your rating was added incorrectly, ask your SR to assist you with this in your appeal.

Sec. 4.29 Ratings for service-connected disabilities requiring hospital treatment or observation.

A total disability rating (100 percent) will be assigned without regard to other provisions of the rating schedule when it is established that a service-connected disability has required hospital treatment in a Department of Veterans Affairs or an approved hospital for a period in excess of 21 days or hospital observation at Department of Veterans Affairs expense for a service-connected disability for a period in excess of 21 days. (a) Subject to the provisions of paragraphs (d), (e), and (f) of this section this increased rating will be effective the first day of continuous hospitalization and will be terminated effective the last day of the month of hospital discharge (regular discharge or release to non-bed care) or effective the last day of the month of termination of treatment or observation for the service-connected disability. A temporary release which is approved by an attending Department of Veterans Affairs physician as part of the treatment plan will not be considered an absence. (1) An authorized absence in excess of 4 days which begins during the first 21 days of hospitalization will be regarded as the equivalent of hospital discharge effective the first day of such authorized absence. An authorized absence of 4 days or less which results in a total of more than 8 days of authorized absence during the first 21 days of hospitalization will be regarded as the equivalent of hospital discharge effective the ninth day of authorized absence. (2) Following a period of hospitalization in excess of 21 days, an authorized absence in excess of 14 days or a third consecutive authorized absence of 14 days will be regarded as the equivalent of hospital discharge and will interrupt hospitalization effective on the last day of the month in which either the authorized absence in excess of 14 days or the third 14 day period begins, except where there is a finding that convalescence is required as provided by paragraph (e) or (f) of this section. The termination of these total ratings will not be subject to Sec. 3.105 (e) of this chapter. (b) Notwithstanding that hospital admission was for disability not connected with service, if during such hospitalization, hospital treatment for a service-connected disability is instituted and continued for a period in excess of 21 days, the increase to a total rating will be granted from the first day of such treatment. If service connection for the disability under treatment is granted after hospital admission, the rating will be from the first day of hospitalization if otherwise in order. (c) The assignment of a total disability rating on the basis of hospital treatment or observation will not preclude the assignment of a total disability rating otherwise in order under other provisions of the rating schedule, and consideration will be given to the propriety of such a rating in all instances and to the propriety of its continuance after discharge. Particular attention, with a view to proper rating under the rating schedule, is to be given to the claims of veterans discharged from hospital, regardless of length of hospitalization, with indications on the final summary of expected confinement to bed or house, or to inability to work with requirement of frequent care of physician or nurse at home. (d) On these total ratings Department of Veterans Affairs regulations governing effective dates for increased benefits will control. (e) The total hospital rating if convalescence is required may be continued for periods of 1, 2, or 3 months in addition to the period provided in paragraph (a) of this section. (f) Extension of periods of 1, 2 or 3 months beyond the initial 3 months may be made upon approval of the Veterans Service Center Manager. (g) Meritorious claims of veterans who are discharged from the hospital with less than the required number of days but need post hospital care and a prolonged period of convalescence will be referred to the Director, Compensation and Pension Service, under Sec. 3.321(b)(1) of this chapter.

- The above section is not known by the majority of Vets that are currently receiving disability compensation or pension or veterans of the Gulf war and current conflicts. If you fit this scenario be sure to follow through on requesting what's due you. An example on how this works; if you were discharged due to an injury obtained while in the service and you are hospitalized for 21 days or more, you would be rated 100% disabled and eligible for disability payments at a rate of 100% temporarily; or if you were in the hospital for 10 days and then you were release but still under observation for another 12 days or more by your primary doctor or a hospital for the same medical injury that sent you to the hospital initially (service connected), you would be 100% disabled and eligible to receive 100% disability rate of pay temporary.

With either of the two scenarios, you could receive 100% rated pay for up to 3 months. If you needed more care, an extension could be approved and you could receive up to an additional 3 months upon approval by the Veterans Service Center Manager or the Director, Compensation and Pension Service. Thereafter your disability would be evaluated to see what your true rating will be. Not a bad deal if you know about it.

I spoke with a SR in my local area and I was told that there's <u>no statute of limitation</u> (the maximum period of time you can file a claim) as to how far back you can go on your claim. Ask a few SR's to get their opinion.

<u>Sec. 4.30 Convalescent ratings</u>.

<u>A total disability rating (100 percent) will be assigned without regard to other provisions of the rating schedule when it is established by report at hospital discharge (regular discharge or release to non-bed care) or outpatient release that entitlement is warranted under paragraph</u> (a) (1), (2) or (3) of this section effective the date of <u>hospital admission or outpatient treatment and continuing for a period of 1, 2, or 3 months from the first day of the month following such hospital discharge or outpatient release</u>. The termination of these total ratings will not be subject to Sec. 3.105 (e) (of this chapter). Such total rating will be followed by appropriate scheduler evaluations. When the evidence is inadequate to assign a scheduler evaluation, a physical examination will be scheduled and considered prior to the termination of a total rating under this section. (a) Total ratings will be assigned under this section if treatment of a service-connected disability resulted in: (1) Surgery necessitating at least one month of convalescence (Effective as to outpatient surgery March 1, 1989.) (2) Surgery with severe postoperative residuals such as incompletely healed surgical wounds, stumps of recent amputations, therapeutic immobilization of one major joint or more, application of a body cast, or the necessity for house confinement, or the necessity for continued use of a wheelchair or crutches (regular weight-bearing prohibited). (Effective as to outpatient surgery March 1, 1989.) (3) Immobilization by cast, without surgery, of one major joint or more. (Effective as to outpatient treatment March 10, 1976.) A reduction in the total rating will not be subject to Sec. 3.105(e) of this chapter. The total rating will be followed by an open rating reflecting the appropriate scheduler evaluation; where the evidence is inadequate to assign the scheduler evaluation, a physical examination will be scheduled prior to the end of the total rating period. (b) A total rating under this section will require full justification on the rating sheet and may be extended as follows: (1) Extensions of 1, 2 or 3 months beyond the initial 3 months may be made under paragraph (a) (1), (2) or (3) of this section. (2) Extensions of 1 or more months up to 6 months beyond the initial 6 months period may be made under paragraph (a) (2) or (3) of this section upon approval of the Veterans Service Center Manager.

- This is a continuance from Sec 4.29 but a little more in detail about the convalescent portion and your disability. This is another bit of information not known to many veterans.

Sec. 4.40 Functional loss.

Disability of the musculoskeletal system is primarily the inability, due to damage or infection in parts of the system, to perform the normal working movements of the body with normal excursion, strength, speed, coordination and endurance. It is essential that the examination on which ratings are based adequately portray the anatomical damage, and the functional loss, with respect to all these elements. The functional loss may be due to absence of part, or all, of the necessary bones, joints and muscles, or associated structures, or to deformity, adhesions, defective innervation, or other pathology, or it may be due to pain, supported by adequate pathology and evidenced by the visible behavior of the claimant undertaking the motion. Weakness is as important as limitation of motion, and a part which becomes painful on use must be regarded as seriously disabled. A little used part of the musculoskeletal system may be expected to show evidence of disuse, either through atrophy, the condition of the skin, absence of normal callosity or the like.

- This section is pretty clear. Just make sure your doctors state your complete limitations and why in your medical file. This goes for any injury that limits your abilities.

Sec. 4.41 History of injury.

In considering the residuals of injury, it is essential to trace the medical-industrial history of the disabled person from the original injury, considering the nature of the injury and the attendant circumstances, and the requirements for, and the effect of, treatment over past periods, and the course of the recovery to date. The duration of the initial, and any subsequent, period of total incapacity, especially periods reflecting delayed union, inflammation, swelling, drainage, or operative intervention, should be given close attention. This consideration, or the absence of clear cut evidence of injury, may result in classifying the disability as not of traumatic origin, either reflecting congenital or developmental etiology, or the effects of healed disease.

- Again, this is pretty straight forward. If you remember earlier I mentioned that the RO in my case only seemed to look at a portion (two years) of the file I submitted, which actually covered over a decade. Based on this guideline they were supposed to go back as far as necessary in order to get a clear picture of the initial injuries history and how it has progressed to date. It is kind of hard to do that by only looking at a few years when you have been disabled over a decade and receiving disability compensation for at least that amount of time. In my case I sited this section in one of my correspondence to the Rating Board.

When I repeatedly speak of acquiring dates for medical records that shows your disability, this section falls right into place. If you specifically show the RO dates and not just send a handful of medical records hoping they will find what you want them to, it should not happen. They will simply send you a correspondence giving you a chance to submit additional evidence, which would extend your waiting period. You stand a better chance giving the information the first time around so that the RO sees the importance of your records, which will lead to you having a better chance of obtaining disability or pension compensation. I will always stress throughout this book, that obtaining copies of your records so that you can review them and to let other doctors see them is very important. Place them in a binder with the oldest reports on the bottom and the most current on top. This way as you update your file the latest reports and exams can simply be placed on top.

Sec. 4.42 Complete medical examination of injury cases.

The importance of complete medical examination of injury cases at the time of first medical examination by the Department of Veterans Affairs cannot be overemphasized. When possible, this should include complete neurological and psychiatric examination, and other special examinations indicated by the physical condition, in addition to the required general and orthopedic or surgical examinations.

- Sometimes, when the Rating Board sends you for an exam, the examiner does not do a good job and it's up to you to let the Rating Board know. As an example; I was sent for a C&P exam (this is simply a compensation exam). The examiner was pleasant but I had issues with the way he performed the exam and the report he made. Examiners are now using a computer program to input information. This way the results can be seen immediately by all authorized personnel. Examiners ask questions and you answer. While he was conducting the exam, I got the feeling he did not know the program very well. At one point he stated, "Oh, I didn't see that" and he left the room for a minute. He was referring to a note at the top of the request asking for a specific condition to be reviewed. One would think a doctor would have reviewed the request in its entirety before you arrive but that seemed not to be the case. As the exam proceeded, I ask if he had records to review and he showed me on the computer screen four medical reports. I ask if that was it and he said yes (examiners should have your complete C-file). I had sent the Rating Board medical records dating from early 1998 to mid-2008. It just goes to show you, if you don't ask question you could possibly be hurting your case. When I received a copy of the report it was totally confusing and in my eye, misrepresented my injuries. When I sent my NOD (Notice of Disagreement) to the Rating Board, don't think I didn't mention my dismay of the exam line by line. Eventually, the Rating Board sent me to a more thorough exam the second time around that lasted 4.5 hours versus the first that only took 1 hour. Now that was an exam. I was checked from the bottom of my feet to the top of my head and the examiner had my C-file to review stretching back 10 years.

There are some important areas that I am appealing and that is the doctor referencing that he did not review private doctor records. This is important in my case because these records show several conditions were caused by my current service connected injuries. So always review your decision with a fine tooth comb. This information that was not reviewed by the doctor could make deference between me being rated 100% versus 90% and unemployable or even obtaining Special Monthly Compensation (SMC) pay on top of my current pay. Ask your SR for more information on SMC pay.

The disabilities VA can consider for SMC include:
- o loss, or loss of use, of a hand or foot
- o immobility of a joint or paralysis
- o loss of sight of an eye (having only light perception)
- o loss, or loss of use, of a reproductive organ
- o complete loss, or loss of use, of both buttocks
- o deafness of both ears (having absence of air and bone conduction)
- o inability to communicate by speech (complete organic aphonia)
- o loss of a percentage of tissue from a single breast, or both breasts, from mastectomy or radiation treatment

Sec. 4.44 The bones.

The osseous abnormalities incident to trauma or disease, such as malunion with deformity throwing abnormal stress upon, and causing malalignment of joint surfaces, should be depicted from study and observation of all available data, beginning with inception of injury or disease, its nature, degree of prostration, treatment and duration of convalescence, and progress of recovery with development of permanent residuals. With shortening of a long bone, some degree of angulations is to be expected; the extent and direction should be brought out by X-ray and observation. The direction of angulations and extent of deformity should be carefully related to strain on the neighboring joints, especially those connected with weight-bearing.

- If you have lower or upper extremity problems make sure you go and see a specialist in that field, even if you're primary doctor is totally competent (knows their field well). As stated throughout this text, make sure your condition is fully diagnosed and written down and placed in your medical file and obtain copies to make sure they are there.

Sec. 4.45 The joints.
As regards the joints the factors of disability reside in reductions of their normal excursion of movements in different planes. Inquiry will be directed to these

considerations: (a) Less movement than normal (due to ankylosis, limitation or blocking, adhesions, tendon-tie-up, contracted scars, etc.). (b) More movement than normal (from flail joint, resections, nonunion of fracture, relaxation of ligaments, etc.). (c) Weakened movement (due to muscle injury, disease or injury of peripheral nerves, divided or lengthened tendons, etc.). (d) Excess fatigability. (e) In coordination, impaired ability to execute skilled movements smoothly. (f) Pain on movement, swelling, deformity or atrophy of disuse. Instability of station, disturbance of locomotion, interference with sitting, standing and weight-bearing is related considerations. For the purpose of rating disability from arthritis, the shoulder, elbow, wrist, hip, knee, and ankle are considered major joints; multiple involvements of the interphalangeal, metacarpal and carpal joints of the upper extremities, the interphalangeal, metatarsal and tarsal joints of the lower extremities, the cervical vertebrae, the dorsal vertebrae, and the lumbar vertebrae, are considered groups of minor joints, ratable on a parity with major joints. The lumbosacral articulation and both sacroiliac joints are considered to be a group of minor joints, ratable on disturbance of lumbar spine functions.

- Same as above, get your doctor to send you to a specialist and make sure they prepare a written diagnosis of your disability.

Sec. 4.46 Accurate measurement.

Accurate measurement of the length of stumps, excursion of joints, dimensions and location of scars with respect to landmarks, should be insisted on. The use of a goniometer in the measurement of limitation of motion is indispensable in examinations conducted within the Department of Veterans Affairs. Muscle atrophy must also be accurately measured and reported.
- Same as above.

Sec. 4.56 Evaluation of muscle disabilities.

(a) An open comminuted fracture with muscle or tendon damage will be rated as a severe injury of the muscle group involved unless, for locations such as in the wrist or over the tibia, evidence establishes that the muscle damage is minimal.
(b) A through-and-through injury with muscle damage shall be evaluated as no less than a moderate injury for each group of muscles damaged.
(c) For VA rating purposes, the cardinal signs and symptoms of muscle disability are loss of power, weakness, lowered threshold of fatigue, fatigue-pain, and impairment of coordination and uncertainty of movement.
(d) Under diagnostic codes 5301 through 5323, disabilities resulting from muscle injuries shall be classified as slight, moderate, moderately severe or severe as follows:

(1) Slight disability of muscles--(i) Type of injury. Simple wound of muscle without debridement or infection.

(ii) History and complaint. Service department record of superficial wound with brief treatment and return to duty. Healing with good functional results. No cardinal signs or symptoms of muscle disability as defined in paragraph (c) of this section.

(iii) Objective findings. Minimal scar. No evidence of fascial defect, atrophy, or impaired tonus. No impairment of function or metallic fragments retained in muscle tissue.

(2) Moderate disability of muscles--(i) Type of injury. Through and through or deep penetrating wound of short track from a single bullet, small shell or shrapnel fragment, without explosive effect of high velocity missile, residuals of debridement, or prolonged infection.

(ii) History and complaint. Service department record or other evidence of in-service treatment for the wound. Record of consistent complaint of one or more of the cardinal signs and symptoms of muscle disability as defined in paragraph (c) of this section, particularly lowered threshold of fatigue after average use, affecting the particular functions controlled by the injured muscles.

(iii) Objective findings. Entrance and (if present) exit scars, small or linear, indicating short track of missile through muscle tissue. Some loss of deep fascia or muscle substance or impairment of muscle tonus and loss of power or lowered threshold of fatigue when compared to the sound side.

(3) Moderately severe disability of muscles--(i) Type of injury. Through and through or deep penetrating wound by small high velocity missile or large low-velocity missile, with debridement, prolonged infection, or sloughing of soft parts, and intermuscular scarring.

(ii) History and complaint. Service department record or other evidence showing hospitalization for a prolonged period for treatment of wound. Record of consistent complaint of cardinal signs and symptoms of muscle disability as defined in paragraph (c) of this section and, if present, evidence of inability to keep up with work requirements.

(iii) Objective findings. Entrance and (if present) exit scars indicating track of missile through one or more muscle groups. Indications on palpation of loss of deep fascia, muscle substance, or normal firm resistance of muscles compared with sound side. Tests of strength and endurance compared with sound side demonstrate positive evidence of impairment.

(4) Severe disability of muscles--(i) Type of injury. Through and through or deep penetrating wound due to high-velocity missile, or large or multiple low velocity missiles, or with shattering bone fracture or open comminuted fracture with extensive debridement, prolonged infection, or sloughing of soft parts, intermuscular binding and scarring.

(ii) History and complaint. Service department record or other evidence showing hospitalization for a prolonged period for treatment of wound. Record of consistent complaint of cardinal signs and symptoms of muscle disability as defined in paragraph

(c) of this section, worse than those shown for moderately severe muscle injuries, and, if present, evidence of inability to keep up with work requirements.

(iii) Objective findings. Ragged, depressed and adherent scars indicating wide damage to muscle groups in missile track. Palpation shows loss of deep fascia or muscle substance, or soft flabby muscles in wound area. Muscles swell and harden abnormally in contraction. Tests of strength, endurance, or coordinated movements compared with the corresponding muscles of the uninjured side indicate severe impairment of function. If present, the following are also signs of severe muscle disability:

(A) X-ray evidence of minute multiple scattered foreign bodies indicating intermuscular trauma and explosive effect of the missile.

(B) Adhesion of scar to one of the long bones, scapula, pelvic bones, sacrum or vertebrae, with epithelial sealing over the bone rather than true skin covering in an area where bone is normally protected by muscle.

(C) Diminished muscle excitability to pulsed electrical current in electrodiagnostic tests.

(D) Visible or measurable atrophy.

(E) Adaptive contraction of an opposing group of muscles.

(F) Atrophy of muscle groups not in the track of the missile, particularly of the trapezius and serratus in wounds of the shoulder girdle.

(G) Induration or atrophy of an entire muscle following simple piercing by a projectile.

- This is just another description as to what an etiology report should cover if your injuries fall under this category.

Sec. 4.57 Static foot deformities.

It is essential to make an initial distinction between bilateral flatfoot as a congenital or as an acquired condition. The congenital condition, with depression of the arch, but no evidence of abnormal callosities, areas of pressure, strain or demonstrable tenderness, is a congenital abnormality which is not compensable or pensionable. In the acquired condition, it is to be remembered that depression of the longitudinal arch, or the degree of depression, is not the essential feature. The attention should be given to anatomical changes, as compared to normal, in the relationship of the foot and leg, particularly to the inward rotation of the superior portion of the os calcis, medial deviation of the insertion of the Achilles tendon, the medial tilting of the upper border of the astragalus. This is an unfavorable mechanical relationship of the parts. A plumb line dropped from the middle of the patella falls inside of the normal point. The forepart of the foot is abducted, and the foot everted. The plantar surface of the foot is painful and shows demonstrable tenderness, and manipulation of the foot produces spasm of the Achilles tendon, peroneal spasm due to adhesion about the peroneal sheaths, and other evidence of pain and limited motion. The symptoms should be apparent without regard to exercise. In severe cases there is gaping of bones on the inner border of the foot, and rigid valgus position with loss of the power of inversion and adduction. Exercise with undeveloped or unbalanced musculature, producing chronic irritation, can be an aggravating factor. In the absence of trauma or other definite evidence of aggravation, service connection is not in order for pes cavus which is a typically congenital or juvenile disease.

- Again, these are areas that need to be covered in your medical file if you have such injuries. I can tell you now that simple x-rays will not show all of the above injury. However, CT or MRI scans will.

Sec. 4.58 Arthritis due to strain.

With service incurred lower extremity amputation or shortening, a disabling arthritis, developing in the same extremity, or in both lower extremities, with indications of earlier, or more severe, arthritis in the injured extremity, including also arthritis of the lumbosacral joints and lumbar spine, if associated with the leg amputation or shortening, will be considered as service incurred, provided, however, that arthritis affecting joints not directly subject to strain as a result of the service incurred amputation will not be granted service connection. This will generally require separate evaluation of the arthritis in the joints directly subject to strain. Amputation, or injury to an upper extremity, is not considered as a causative factor with subsequently developing arthritis, except in joints subject to direct strain or actually injured.

- Though this section speaks of amputation, there are other forms of arthritis that are compensable under multiple rating codes for joints not amputated such as, osteoarthritis.

Sec. 4.59 Painful motion.

With any form of arthritis, painful motion is an important factor of disability, the facial expression, wincing, etc., on pressure or manipulation, should be carefully noted and definitely related to affected joints. Muscle spasm will greatly assist the identification. Sciatic neuritis is not uncommonly caused by arthritis of the spine. The intent of the schedule is to recognize painful motion with joint or periarticular pathology as productive of disability. It is the intention to recognize actually painful, unstable, or malaligned joints, due to healed injury, as entitled to at least the minimum compensable rating for the joint. Crepitation either in the soft tissues such as the tendons or ligaments, or crepitation within the joint structures should be noted carefully as points of contact which are diseased. Flexion elicits such manifestations. The joints involved should be tested for pain on both active and passive motion, in weight-bearing and nonweight-bearing and, if possible, with the range of the opposite undamaged joint.

- This is very important. Many times when you have arthritis, it has been diagnosed based on imaging photographs i.e., x-rays, CT Scans, Ultrasound and Dobbler test. When your doctors pull you in to review the outcome of these tests, make sure you express all ailments, pains etc., you feel. They need to know the full range of your complications. Make sure you ask them to place the entire diagnosis in your medical file with a comparison to your service related injury. It is important that your doctors express their finding in written form and reference the possibility that likely or not it was caused by your service connected injury. I am being repetitive on this point because it can make or break your case.

Sec. 4.61 Examination.

With any form of arthritis (except traumatic arthritis) it is essential that the examination for rating purposes cover all major joints, with especial reference to Heberden's or Haygarth's nodes.

Sec. 4.62 Circulatory disturbances.

The circulatory disturbances, especially of the lower extremity following injury in the popliteal space, must not be overlooked, and require rating generally as phlebitis.

Sec. 4.63 Loss of use of hand or foot.

Loss of use of a hand or a foot, for the purpose of special monthly compensation, will be held to exist when no effective function remains other than that which would be equally well served by an amputation stump at the site of election below elbow or knee with use of a suitable prosthetic appliance. The determination will be made on the basis of the actual remaining function of the hand or foot, whether the acts of grasping, manipulation, etc., in the case of the hand, or of balance and propulsion, etc., in the case of the foot, could be accomplished equally well by an amputation stump with prosthesis.

   a. Extremely unfavorable complete ankylosis of the knee, or complete ankylosis of 2 major joints of an extremity, or shortening of the lower extremity of 3\1/2\ inches (8.9 cms.) or more, will be taken as loss of use of the hand or foot involved.
   b. Complete paralysis of the external popliteal nerve (common peroneal) and consequent, footdrop, accompanied by characteristic organic changes including trophic and circulatory disturbances and other concomitants confirmatory of complete paralysis of this nerve, will be taken as loss of use of the foot.

   This basically states what I covered above under Sec 4.59.

Sec. 4.70 Inadequate examinations.

If the report of examination is inadequate as a basis for the required consideration of service connection and evaluation, the rating agency may request a supplementary report from the examiner giving further details as to the limitations of the disabled person's ordinary activity imposed by the disease, injury, or residual condition, the prognosis for return to, or continuance of, useful work. When the best interests of the service will be advanced by personal conference with the examiner, such conference may be arranged through channels.

The above sections have been placed in this book to help you get a good idea on how the RO looks upon a compensation case. This list of sections that I have compiled is for your benefit. Some on this list may concern you and some may not. The main thing is to show your doctors exactly what is needed in their etiology report. It is much better to show them what is needed then to hope that they get it right. Doctors really hate it when you come back more than once to ask for a more detailed report when you could have given them a guideline as to what was needed the first time. If you have a private doctor, chances are they will charge you for a report the first time and are definitely going to charge you again if more work is needed.

If you did not see your condition listed above, do not worry. I am simply trying to give a starting point of reference for your physician in order for them to create a complete report on your condition(s). You can use the same format on just about any injury whether eye, heart, the female anatomy etc. Simply read Part 4 in its entirety at the website mentioned under THINGS YOU MAY NOT HAVE KNOWN. You can locate the particular condition you have in Title 38 Part 4 and give the information to your doctor along with the list that I have placed above.

Now we will look at putting everything that we have discussed into motion. I know the beginning of this text is tedious and possibly boring to read but it is important for you to understand how the Rating Board system works and why a lot of veterans get denied on their first and sometimes second request. When I first put my case together, I thought back to when I prepared business plans. I always used the old school five W's for the groundwork. This system works great for a lot of different scenarios.

- **Who:** Who are the authorities handling my case file and who makes the final decision?
- **What:** What is expected of me, the veteran? What documents need to be gathered and submitted? What time limits do I have?
- **When:** When do I submit the case file and when will I hear from the VA?
- **Where**: Where do I send my request and where can I find assistance to help me?
- **Why**: Why are requests denied the first time around or why was my rating so low?

If you apply this thought process when putting your case together, your chance of receiving benefits has greatly increased. In order to satisfy these questions you need to understand what is expected of you. Understanding the above sections in this chapter prepares you for that. Look through Title 38 - Part 3 and especially Part 4. Both Parts work together. Beyond giving information on receiving compensation, Part 3 offers information about what else may be available to you and your family.

How are we going to begin the process? Well, the first thing is to know what to do versus what not to do. There are some areas that I need to pound into your head.

What To Do

- Sign up with a SR in your area to assist you. Let him/her know what you are attempting to do and where your case stands at the present if you started on your own. If you have received letters from the VA referencing your case, make sure to take a copy with you to your first appointment along with any letters you have written to the VA and your DD214. Also let the SR know what medical documentation you have sent. It's never too late to sign up with a SR. The SR will want to start a file on you. You want to make sure that you have not been using the wrong verbiage or sending the wrong information to the VA. In short you want to make sure that the SR is updated on your case. You might want to take a copy of your medical records if you have them. They can make copies for you to save on money and place in your file what they consider to be important documents.

- If you already receive disability benefits and are requesting an increase in rating or appealing a current decision, request a copy of your C-File if you have not done so yet and all other private and VA medical records not in your possession. If this is a new request, your C-File will only have medical records from the service if any. Your Regional VA Office or your SR can assist you. You can order your own health records by filling out **VA Form 10-5345a Individual's Request For A Copy Of Their Own Health Information**. Don't be surprised depending upon your age if you receive a letter stating that no records were found or available. Due to a fire in the past at the main record facility that housed all VA records, many Vets lost valuable information. To request a copy of your military records and DD 214 use VA Form SF 180, which can be downloaded from my website?

- After receiving a copy of your DD-214, you can take it down to the County Recorder's Office and they can record it. In case you lose your copy you can go back to the county office and get a copy rather than waiting for the VA to send it. There may be a time when you need it immediately. Be careful if you decide to do this because of the abuse of personal information being released or stolen. The choice is yours to decide.

- Build a relationship with your doctors if you have not already. They are not your enemy and ask questions. You want them to work with you and not against you. Being polite goes a long way. Remember, they are the ones that will write your etiology reports. Most VA and private doctors work 8 hours per day. That means that they would have to complete your report after hours because of their daily busy schedules. Ask your current doctors to write an etiology based reports on your current medical condition(s) that you feel are service connected. VA and/or private doctor reports carry all the weight when it comes to the Rating Board. Let them know what you are doing and give them a copy of the Title 38 section list, which shows what the VA is looking for in a report. If you get the report right the first time around, your review by the Rating Board will move much faster. You must have the doctors' review your past as well as your current medical records that you have accumulated on your perceived service injury and make sure that in their report it states that they have reviewed "past and present records". **(In Nieves-Rodriguez v. Peake, 22 Vet. App. 295 (2008), the Court found that a medical opinion that contains only data and conclusions is accorded no weight**). The reason behind this statement is when a RO reviews your case file they look to see if doctors have actually reviewed both your past and present medical history and has wrote a full descriptive medical report. As an example; if you are sent for an exam by the VA, the examiner is supposed to have your C-file and other private medical records you've submitted with your application for their review. They will write a report based on that information and the current findings of the physical exam. They will also mention that they have reviewed past records. At the same time, if you have a private doctor write a report and there is no mention of them reviewing your past medical records, when it comes down to which reports the RO will give more wait to or accept might be the one from the VA examiner. Why? The RO will give more weight towards the VA report because that examiner will always state they reviewed past medical records, whereas the private doctor had no mention of reviewing your past records. *Small details such as this can hurt your case tremendously.* If the report from the VA examiner is negative (meaning they feel your condition is not service related) and the report from your private doctors is positive (making statements to the effect that your condition is service related) more weight will be given to the VA report just because they reviewed your past records. Had the private doctor mentioned reviewing your records a reasonable doubt would have arouse and your private doctors report should be given more weight over the VA's based on "**Title 38 Sec. 4.3 Resolution of reasonable doubt**" and further explained in **Title 38 Part 3 Sec 3.102** . The only other way the doctors report would carry more weight would be if you have been under the care of this physician for multiple years and they state so. This would show that you have had a physician who knows your medical history well over the past several years. Earlier in this reading under Important Websites, I spoke of Vets reviewing past appeal claims so that they can see how the BVA looks at cases. You will see a lot of times when the BVA over turns a negative decision based on VA C&P exam, the BVA gave more wait to the private and VA primary physician reports because the Vet had been under their care for long periods of time rather than a one day exam performed by the VA. Their knowledge of you, should over shadow a onetime exam by a VA C&P examiner. Do you get the meaning of the above?

Always review your med records as soon as possible to make sure your reports are in order.

- Ask your doctors are there any further test you can take to find out a clearer picture of your medical condition i.e., CT scans, MRI's, Ultra Sound, Dobbler etc.

- After receiving all of your VA medical record, make a copy for your private physician(s) if you have one. This way if you forget to mention a condition, you and your private physician have something to reference to. Build a file with your current documents on top descending down to the oldest on the bottom. Use form 21-4138 Statement In Support Of Claim to let the Rating Board know what you are seeking. If you need additional space, just take a second 21-4138 and continue writing. Remember to write down descriptions, places and dates of records showing your disability. If you can remember some of the GI's names that were around when you were injured, make sure you mention them and the circumstances around becoming injured. Remember, a lot of military records were destroyed in the fire at the main VA holding facility where military records where held in the past. In those cases the Rating Board has to rely on the information that you give them. I have prepared for your use a standard form, which can be used to record all of your medical appointments. You can find this form on my website.

- Fill out and attach the Certification of Fully Developed Claim form. This is a new form required by the VA to be submitted with all claims. This is part of a pilot program which tries to clear cases within a 90 day period based on a fully completed application package. Try to do everything right the first time to save on downtime. If you miss something major the RO will ask for you to submit the additional information and will give you a time limit to do so. This will possibly add another three months or more to your waiting period.

What Not To Do

- Do not become angry with your VA doctors, when after reviewing your clinical reports they are not as descriptive as you would like. If you have a problem with these doctors not wanting to assist you, each VA facility has a Veteran's Advocate that will be more than willing to assist you with your needs.

- VA does not like making multiple copies of your full medical or C-file records over and over again, so make sure you order all the necessary records the first time around. They will however have no problem updating records. Never give your original records to anyone to keep.

- When talking to your doctor, do not make it seem like you are telling them how to do their job. Just explain the urgency of having a detailed report. Simply show them the Title 38 list, which gives them a guideline to go off of. It states exactly what you want them to know in order to write an etiology report. Again, if you have problems with VA doctors, speak with the VA advocate in your local area.

- When speaking with a SR, don't act like you know more than him/her. You want them to help you so be curdiest.

- Don't send in unorganized files to the Rating Board. If they cannot find what they are looking for because the file is junky, your file will most likely be set aside and worked on later. You will never know, so do not take that chance. Be as organized as possible. Take the time to purchase a relatively cheap binder for $2.00 - $5.00 to place your documents in.

To put the above comments into perspective, you need to understand that submitting a case file to the rating agency in an organized manor will be appreciated by the Rating Board and will make it easier for them to review the facts of your case.

You also have to become educated on the workings of the Rating Board system so that you know when you submit your file it has all the necessary documents for a fair review by the Rating Board the first time around.

I mentioned C-files previously. These are records that contain personnel and medical records from when you first entered the Armed Forces to your discharge. It will also have records associated with a current compensation case if you have one. It's important for every veteran to obtain a copy of their C-file. If you are single or married with children and something happens to you where you cannot function without assistance, whomever you have delegated as your caregiver should have access to your records so that they can obtain additional help for you and your family if you are or become eligible for services offered by the VA. Having access to your records and obtaining assistance from a SR would allow the caregiver or your spouse to find out if there is any benefits/assistance available. Make sure you have a Medical Power of Attorney signed an submitted to your local VA medical center in case you become so medically out of it that the chosen caregiver can make medical decision for you on your behalf.

Another important factor for having a copy of your C-File is, you may have had a condition that started prior to entering the service and it was notated in your medical records or while you were on active duty, it might show a medical condition that was acquired at some point and time while enlisted. In that case, you could possibly receive disability benefits based on that medical condition. If you are an older Vet or have memory problems, it is not unusual to have forgotten injuries that you obtained while in service. Remember, while in service you were government property. So if you were playing for the company basketball team and ended up tearing a ligament, this would be a service related injury. I got you thinking now.

The VA has what it calls "presumptive periods". If you have a disability that becomes visible within a 1 year period from the date you were discharged from service and you can prove you contracted this medical problem while in service or you aggravated/irritated an existing injury that you had prior to entering the service, you could possibly be eligible to receive compensation for that injury. There have also been cases approved where the medical injury showed itself several years after discharge. One such disease is diabetes.

Service men that actually set foot in Vietnam may have been exposed to Agent Orange. The VA assumes if you were in Vietnam and you now are a diabetic, you may claim disability for diabetes based on being exposed to Agent Orange. For Vets that were or are in a current engagement, the VA has been working towards assisting these Vets because of unknown diseases they have contracted. Check with a SR for further information on these type of cases. The amount of compensation is dependent upon how severe the disease affects you. Also, if you were in the Navy or stationed on a ship or PT boat that patrolled certain areas in Vietnam, you could also be eligible under the same scenario as stated above.

3.313 Claims based on service in Vietnam.

(a) Service in Vietnam. "Service in Vietnam" includes service in the waters offshore or service in other locations if the conditions of service involved duty or visitation in Vietnam.
This eligibility was instated in 2010, so check with a SR for more information if you were in the Navy.

One other injury that has a delayed appearance is cold weather injuries. Again, it could be several years before you really feel the effects from this injury. If you are one of the unlucky Vets that fall under this category, make sure you see a physician (private and VA) that specializes in cold weather injuries. Cold injuries affect the neurological, circulatory systems and causes edema. Many physicians are aware of cold injuries but they really cannot comprehend the multiple complications that are associated with these types of injuries. Bottom line, whatever your condition is fine a specialist.

To this point we have gone over items that you need for submission. Now let's go through our check list and put these documents together:

1. Have you signed up with a SR?
2. Have you ordered a copy of your C-file and current medical records (private and VA)? Remember to make a copy of your records or have them scanned and placed on a disc.
3. Have you spoke with your primary VA and/or private doctor(s) to see if there are any additional tests you can take to define your injury i.e., CT scan, MRI, Ultra Sound, Dobbler test etc. ?
4. Have you ask your VA and/or private doctor(s) to write an etiology based report on your current medical condition? Did you give your private doctor, if you have one, a copy of your medical records and the Title 38 section list, which can be downloaded from my website?
5. Have you requested letters from relatives, co-workers and employers talking about how they have seen your medical condition(s) affect your ability to function with everyday life and the ability to work? Did they notice any restriction from your daily activities etc.?
6. For individuals that are exiting the Armed Services with a disability, the VA has initiated a program to assist serviceman with their disability case prior to their departing the service. This process is called the Disability Evaluation System (DES) and it operates under public law (Title 10 and Title 38) to ensure you are treated fairly. You can read the entire procedure referencing service men and women existing in the Armed Forces with service related injuries at: http://www.turbotap.org/portal/transition/resources/PDF/Compensation_and_Ben efits_Handbook.pdf

New Submission	Description
msoB3 Certification of Fully Developed Claim VA Form 21-0844	This is a new form placed into circulation December 2008 in part of a pilot program which is attempting to complete review of case files within a 90 day period from the date of a fully submitted file to the VA for compensation cases.
VBA-21-526-ARE Pension & Disability	This is the application for new disability and pension claims
VBA-21-4138-ARE Statement In Support of Claim	This form is used to fully describe your injury(ies) and what you are requesting, i.e., new submission, higher rating or appealing a decision
DD214	Separation Documentation
Disagreement with Decision	**Description**
NOD (Notice of Disagreement)	If you disagree with a decision you will be instructed by the VA to submit a NOD as a part of the appeals process. This is a hand written letter addressing your disagreement
msoB3 Certification of Fully Developed Claim VA Form 21-0844	As stated above
Request for Higher Rating	**Description**
msoB3 Certification of Fully Developed Claim VA Form 21-0844	As stated above
VBA-21-4138-ARE Statement In Support of Claim	As stated Above
Form 21-8940 Veterans Application for Increased Compensation Based on Unemployability	If you are stating that you are unemployable, then this form is needed
Appeals	**Description**
Form 9	After receiving a Statement of the Case form the VA, if you decide to appeal your case you would have to fill this form out
VBA-21-4138-ARE Statement In Support of Claim	
Health benefits	**Description**

VHA-10-10ez app for health benefits	If you are not enrolled with the VA healthcare system to receive medical care, fill this form out and take it to your local VA clinic. If you have not been rated yet, the VA will base your care on your income status

In all of the following cases, at some point and time, you will receive a Development letter stating; your rights, what the VA will do to assist you and a form asking you if you need additional time to submit more information or if you want them to decide your case with the information on hand.

Now that we know what needs to be in your file, let us begin to put the file together. Before you start packaging your case file, make sure you fully know what you want first. If you feel you are unemployable due to service related injuries, apply for it at the onset. I have heard Vets state that some of the organization that assist them file claims for individual injuries first in order to have them meet the minimum requirements to be eligible for unemployability. When the Rating Board reviews your case, prior to looking at unemployability, they will first rate your singular or multiple injuries. Once you have meet the minimum rating requirements for unemployability the board will then review your qualifications for unemployability to see if you meet those standards. Remember, if you submit a file in its entirety the first time around you will save a lot of downtime waiting for a decision. If on the other hand you have already submitted your file and you decide you want to apply for unemployability, speak with your SR first. I'm quite sure they will want you to wait until your first rating has been finalized. Submitted additional request later in the game will delay both request. I've been told by numerous SR's that if one department of the Rating Board has to request a copy of the C-file already being reviewed for a case, all work on that file will stop until the file has been copied and reviewed to facilitate the later request. In short you will extend your waiting time until both requests are settled

New Submissions

You want to stack it in a similar manner as shown below
1. Place all private medical files in the binder first with the most recent records on top descending down to the oldest on the bottom. **Submit medical records that pertain to your service related injuries only**
2. Next place all medical research reports (*only if you want to. This is not mandatory. This takes a lot of reading on your part*) that you are using as laymen evidence. This will help show the nexus (how one injury affects another) between your injuries.
3. Next place all etiology reports (detailed medical reports referencing your

condition) obtained from VA and private doctors.

4. Next place all letters from relatives, friends, past employers and co-workers.

5. Next place the form that I formatted for your use to show dates, places and a brief description of your injuries.

6. Next place a copy of your marriage certificate if married. If you have children the main application for compensation will ask for their social security numbers and ages of each child. If you care for an elderly or disabled parent, submit proof they live with you and you are caring for them.

7. Next place your DD214. When I was discharged, I received two DD214's. One was for my initial enlistment and the second was for my re-enlistment, so submit all DD214's.

8. Next place VA Form VBA-21-526-ARE Pension & Disability. This is your application for compensation.

9. Next place VA Form 21-4138 Statement In Support Of Claim. In this document you will explain what your disabilities are; your medical problems associated with your service related injury(ies), why you think these injuries are service related, how does your injury affect your ability to work and perform everyday task, how does these injuries affect you physically as well as mentally, how long have you had the injuries, when did they occur and under what circumstances, state the name – rank of anyone that was around when the injury happened and where etc. Basically, tell the entire story of the injury. Do not leave anything out. You never know what is important or not. Let the Rating Board know exactly how you feel from morning until evening. What is your normal daily activity like? Are you in pain constantly? If you walk with a cane or have prosthetic devices let them know. Do you need help putting on such devices? Can you feed yourself or do you need assistance? Do you need help bathing or brushing your teeth? If they do not know what is going on in your life as it pertains to the injuries, they cannot picture your disability. Use my letters "**ONLY**" as a guide. Your circumstances may defer from mine but the letters still gives you a starting point of reference. **Note: Remember to use the proper verbiage of the secondary injuries, i.e. aggravated or caused by as expressed under "Sec. 4.9 Congenital or developmental defects."**

10. Last but not least place VA Form msoB3 Certification of Fully Developed Claim. Here you will give a brief description as to what you are seeking and reference all other information on VA Form 21-4138 Statement In Support Of Claim. You can view my letters in later chapters.

Now we will look at what is needed for a higher rating request and its stacking order. This is basically the same as a new submission. The following may be repetitive but it will assure that you have the right documents for submission.

1. Place all private medical files in the binder as described above.

2. Next place all medical research documentation.
3. Next place all doctor etiology reports.
4. Next place all letters from relatives, friends, past employers and co-workers.
5. Next place the form that I formatted for your use.
6. If you are claiming unemployability then you will submit Form 21-8940 Veterans Application for Increased Compensation Based on Unemployability.
7. Next place VA Form 21-4138 Statement In Support Of Claim. Use the same information as shown above.
8. Last but not least place VA Form msoB3 Certification of Fully Developed Claim.

It is not much deferent than the new submission documentation. I just need to make sure there is no confusion between any of the submission documents.

Now we will discuss the process when you disagree with a decision made by the VA (an appeal). As examples, I will be using my personal case showing you copies of some of my submission letters and other documents sent to the VA.

We will first look at the 7 step process explaining how things work. This will give you a good idea on the process from start to finish. This information was obtained from http://www.military.com. This website additionally gives an outlook on VA benefits just like the main VA website.

7 steps to an appeal:

Step 1. The first step in the appeal process is for a claimant to file a written appeal with the local VA regional office or medical center that made the decision. This is not a special form; it is simply your hand written statement that (1) you disagree with your local VA office's claim determination, and (2) you want to appeal it.

Submit your appeal to the same local VA office that issued the decision you are appealing. If you have moved and your claims file is now maintained at a local VA office other than the one where you previously filed you claim, submit your appeal to the new location.

If you have received notice of determinations on more than one claim issue, be specific about which issue or issues you are appealing. For example, if your local VA office made claim decisions on your pension and a medical payment, but you only want to appeal the decision on your medical payment, be sure to note that.

Note: You may have the option to elect a Decision Review Officer (DRO) instead of the traditional full Board of Appeals review. In most "clear error of omission" cases, the DRO process tends to save time and processing for both you and the VA.

This is an informal appellate process within the regional office. The DRO has the authority to reverse or modify a VA Rating Board decision. We recommend that you seek DRO review before you request a BVA appeal. The DRO process is frequently successful and is generally faster than going straight to the BVA. If you do not receive a better decision from the DRO, you can still appeal to the BVA.

Step 2. After receiving the appeal, the VA will mail the claimant (the Vet) a Statement of the Case describing what facts, laws and regulations were used in deciding the case. A VA Form 9 (Appeal to the Board of Veterans Appeals (http://www4.va.gov/vaforms/va/pdf/VA9.pdf) will be included with the Statement of the Case.

If you wish to continue your appeal, you must complete and submit the VA Form 9 within 30-60 days of the mailing of the Statement of the Case, or within one year from the date the VA mailed its decision, whichever is later. Send your VA Form 9 to the local VA office handling your case; the office will file this and all related information in a claims folder, and will eventually forward it to the Board of Veterans Appeals for review.

On VA Form 9, make sure you clearly state the benefit you want and point out any mistakes you think the VA has made in its decision. If you submit new information or evidence with your VA Form 9, your local VA office, and it will prepare a Supplemental Statement of the Case (SSOC). If you are not satisfied with the SSOC, you have 60 days from the date the SSOC was mailed to submit, in writing, what you disagree with.

Usually, the above is all the paperwork you will need to send to your VA office. The one major exception is if you receive a SSOC covering a new issue. In this case, you must complete a supplemental VA Form 9 covering the new issue if you want to appeal it. For example, if you are appealing a pension ruling, and before the pension ruling is resolved, you appeal a medical payment ruling and receive an SSOC on the medical payment decision, you must send your VA office a VA Form 9 on the medical payment appeal.

It is possible to get an extension for the 60-day window you have to submit your VA Form 9 or respond to the SSOC. Simply write to your local VA office handling your appeal and explain why you need extra time to file.

Step 3. You can represent yourself in your appeal if you wish, but most people who appeal obtain representation. You can choose to be represented by a Veteran's Service Organization (VSO) or your state's veterans department. Most VSO's have trained personnel who specialize in providing help with claims and appeals. Your local VA office can provide a list of approved veterans appeal representatives in your area.

You can also be represented by a private lawyer or recognized agent. If you want representation, fill out a VA Form 21-22 to authorize a VSO to represent you, or use VA Form 22a to authorize an attorney or recognized agent to represent you.

Step 4. Once you have filed your appeal with your local VA office, it will be forwarded to the Board of Veterans' Appeals (BVA). Your VA office will send you a letter when they receive your claims folder. You have 90 days from the mailing date of this letter, or when the Board decides your case (whichever comes first) to add more evidence to your file, request a hearing (see Step Five) or select/change your representative (See Step Three).

If you need to submit any of these items after the 90 days are up, you must submit a written request to the Board, with an explanation for why the item(s) are late.

Until your file is transferred to the Board, your local VA office is the best place to get information about your appeal. After your file has been transferred, you can call (202) 565-5436 to check on its status.

The Board processes appeals files in the order received. It will assign your case a docket number. For example, if your appeal was the very first appeal to be reviewed in the year 1999, it would have docket number 99-00001. Thus, the larger your docket number, the longer you may have to wait for your case to be reviewed.

On average, you may have to wait two or more years after you file your appeal for the Board to pass a final decision on your case. Complex cases may take longer. If you want your appeal to be reviewed sooner, you can try writing directly to the Board and explain the reasons why you need a quicker ruling. Write to this address:

Board of Veterans' Appeals (014)
Department of Veterans Affairs
810 Vermont Ave., NW
Washington, DC 20420

You will need "convincing proof of exceptional circumstances," which includes situations such as terminal illness, danger of bankruptcy or foreclosure, or an error by the VA that caused a significant delay in the docketing of your appeal. Be sure to provide evidence (i.e., bankruptcy notices) if you have it.

Step 5. If you wish, you can also have a personal hearing. A personal hearing is a meeting between you (and your legal representative, if you have one) and a VA official who will decide your case. During this meeting, you present testimony and other evidence supporting your case. There are two types of personal hearings: local office hearings and BVA hearings.

A local office hearing is held at your local VA office between you and a "hearing officer" from the local office's staff. To arrange a local office hearing, you should contact your local VA office or your appeal representative as early in the appeal process as possible.

In addition to a local office hearing, you have the right to present your case in person to a member of the Board of Veterans' Appeals (a BVA hearing). In most parts of the U.S., you can choose whether to hold this hearing at your local VA office, or at the BVA office in Washington, DC (but not both).

To request a BVA hearing, check the appropriate box on VA Form 9. If you have already submitted your VA Form 9 without checking the box, you can request a hearing by writing directly to the Board of Veterans' Appeals within 90 days. Be sure you clearly state whether you want the hearing held at your local VA office or in Washington. Please note that the BVA cannot pay for any expenses — such as lodging or travel — in connection with a hearing.

Basically, to "testify" at a BVA hearing just means to tell what you know about your case. VA hearings are much more informal than court hearings, so you don't need to worry about technical rules of evidence or being cross-examined when you testify.

Some local offices offer video teleconferencing, so you can have your BVA hearing at your local office while the BVA member talks to you from Washington. Check with your local VA office to see if it offers this option.

Be aware that a personal hearing may take some time to arrange. Most BVA hearings are held about three months before the case is actually reviewed by the Board.

Step 6. The Board will notify you when it receives your appeal from the local VA office. When the docket number for your appeal is reached, your file will be examined by a Board member and a staff attorney who will check it for completeness, and review all the evidence, your arguments, personal hearing transcripts (if any), the statement of your representative (if you have one) and any other information.

Once a decision has been reached, the Board will notify you in writing. Your decision will be mailed to your home address, so it is extremely important you keep the VA informed of your current address.

If the claimant dies before the Board makes a final decision, the Board normally dismisses the appeal without issuing a decision. The rights of the deceased claimant's survivors are not affected by this action. Survivors may still file a claim at the local VA office for any benefits to which they may be entitled.

Sometimes the Board will remand an appeal, which means it returns the case to your local VA office with instructions for additional work to be done. Remands may occur because of changes in the law, or if you do (or don't do) certain things.

After your local VA office performs whatever additional work is necessary, it will review your case and issue a new decision. If its original ruling still holds, it will send the case back to the Board for a final decision. The case keeps its original place on the Board's docket, so it will be reviewed soon after the Board receives it.

Step 7. If you disagree with the Board's final ruling, you can appeal to the U.S. Court of Veterans Appeals for Veterans Claims. Normally, you must file a Notice of Appeal with the Court within 120 days from the date the Board's decision is mailed to you.

To get more information about the Notice of Appeal, methods for filing with the Court, Court filing fees and other related matters, you can call the Court at 1-800-869-8654 or write to the address below:

United States Court of Appeals for Veterans Claims
625 Indiana Ave, NW, Suite 900
Washington, DC 20004
Telephone: (202) 501-5970

If you appeal to the Court, you should also file a copy of the Notice of Appeal with the VA General Counsel at the following address:

Office of the General Counsel (027)
Department of Veterans Affairs
810 Vermont Ave., NW
Washington, DC 20420

There are other ways to challenge the Board's decision:

Motion for Reconsideration — If you can prove that the Board made an obvious error of fact or law in its decision, you can file a written motion for reconsideration. If you have a representative, you should consult with him/her about whether you should file a motion.

Reopening the Case — If you have new evidence, you can request that your case be re-opened. To be considered, the evidence you submit must include information related to your case that was not included in your claims folder when the Board decided your case. To re-open your case, you need to submit your new evidence directly to your local VA office.

CUE Motion — A Board decision can be reversed or revised if you can prove that the decision contained "clear and unmistakable error" (CUE). Because CUE is a very complicated area of law, you should ask your representative for advice before you decide to file a CUE motion. You can file a CUE motion at any time, but if you file it after filing a Notice of Appeal with the U.S. Court of Appeals for Veterans Claims, the Board cannot rule on your CUE motion. CUE motions should be filed directly with the Board, and not your local VA office. Consult your SR first before submitting any documents.

Here is your stacking order for the above accept for a CUE.
1. Place all new VA and private medical records evidence in the binder.
2. Next place all new material evidence coming from medical research documentation.
3. Next place all new doctor etiology reports.
4. Next place VA Form 21-4138 Statement In Support Of Claim.
5. Next place VA Form msoB3 Certification of Fully Developed Claim.
   a. Next place your Notice of Disagreement. Again, this is not a special form; it is simply your written statement that (1) you disagree with your local VA office's claim determination, and (2) the decision contained "clear and unmistakable error" (CUE). Be very specific when describing your concerns.

This concludes how to package your specific case file. I mentioned earlier that you can verify this information when you sign up with a SR, plus you can go directly to the sources websites that I have enclosed in the book and read the information directly from the website that the information came from. There is nothing better than getting information directly from the source.

Note: Make sure you request everything that you want the first time around. If you add additional conditions or expand on the initial request, you will delay the processing of your claim.

Now we will look at my case along with some of my submission letters to the VA that can be used as reference points "**ONLY**" when writing your correspondence. If you have problems typing letters because of arthritis etc., buy a dictation machine. A dictation machine can be purchased for as little as $20.00 or less.

The first letter is the initial request I sent to receive a higher rating. The only changes made from the original letters are some grammar errors. The body of the letters is exactly the same. When reviewing the letters, I have found some items that should not have been expressed in such long terms. These specific items are the verbiage used within each section that I quoted coming from Title 38 Part 4. In your letters, simply put the section numbers in without placing what they say. Each RO has access to Title 38, so keep this portion as short as possible. Also, I retrieved medical information directly from medical websites. With each of my injuries that I was requesting compensation for, I was attempting to show a nexus (a comparison) between each injury. For some reason the RO and the DRO did not give this any wait. I felt this was valid because the laws governing the Rating Board give you the opportunity to submit laymen evidence. Why offer us Vets this opportunity and not give it any weight. What I found out after doing a little more research was if your medical records do not use some of the same terminology, so far as, showing a link between your service related injury and the laymen evidence then no wait is given toward your claim. At least that's the way I looked at it. This is kind of a catch 22. The laws governing compensation says you can submit such evidence but the Rating Board will not comment as to why such evidence was or was not acceptable. *This is just something to be aware of when submitting laymen eviden*ce. I think from here on out, you should take what you found doing your research and show it to your physicians first. Get them to comment on the research and see what they think. There is a possibility that they can incorporate some of the verbiage in your report.

When I received my first SOC (Statement of Case) from the Rating Board, they only mentioned that they had reviewed the information but made no comment to its acceptance thereof or not. Makes you wonder if they ever read your entire case file or maybe you just simply missed something. I would still submit this information in your file. You might get a RO that looks at it more than others would. Different personalities see things in a different light. It's simple nature 101.

First initial request

I am requesting that my current disability rating be re-evaluated due to my deteriorating disabilities over the past 10 years. I have attempted to hold down employment but I have *had to take off an overwhelming amount of time due to my lower extremities and other medical problems. I had begun the process in 1999 requesting a re-evaluation for my current rating at that time. I obtain the assistance of the (**Blocked due to legalities**) in keeping my case open. I had a time limit in submitting evidence, which the required document was faxed to the proper VA department. Approximately a month later I found out that the document was not received in a timely manner. I know we faxed it on time so I requested a copy of the doc that was received by the VA to see the fax date stamp that should have shown up on either the top of the document or bottom but it did not show. I rather received a single page showing a received date some 20 days after my time had expired. This was devastating since I had spent a lot of time and energy in staying in compliance and was applying for unemployability. Since this meant starting all over again, I was forced to work at a convenience store where I lasted 3 months before quitting. The pain that I endured standing on my feet just could not be taken anymore plus I was getting infections again.*

Since my first initial rating, I have experienced more severe cellulites infections in my lower extremities, as well as more agonizing pain radiating from my feet up through my thighs and from my back down my legs. I have seen nerve doctors and podiatrist. All finding are within the enclosed documents. The last VA foot doctor I seen stated that there was nothing else he could do for me and that my symptoms would worsen over the years. He did attempt to send me through therapy but again I was told by that department they could not help either. I presently wear joist stockings and orthopedic footwear. I now have more new onset conditions, which has caused additional medical problems such as, numinous in my left big toe, upper right thigh, bottom right heel, severe neuropathy damage, heel spurs, hammer toe and a return venous problem with lower extremities. I have also had to deal with other medical problems as listed. Examples are degenerative disc disease, which exasperates the pain in my lower extremities, hyperlipidemia, insulin dependent diabetes, depression, stress, migraine headaches, fatigue, a distal hernia, acid reflux, vertigo, arthritis and a weak knee from an injury that occurred in 1979 during company basketball practice Ft Ord, CA. I do feel they all play apart with my current service connected disability as to the pain I have to endure. Below is a list of time frames in which infections have set in. All records in reference to these illnesses are enclosed.

- *Salinas Valley Memorial (SMV) Hosp Salinas, CA (Cellulites). An initial infection set in on 03/98. Antibiotics were given and the infection subsides for a few months. 10/98 I was admitted after getting seriously ill while at work. My wife took me to the emergency ward of SMV where I was admitted for a cellulites infection in my lower extremity. I stayed in the hospital for approximately 4 days. After my release I was given an additional 10 days worth of antibiotics to clear the infection.*

- *Salinas Valley Memorial (SMV) Hosp Salinas, CA (chest pains). Hospitalized for 4 days on 01/1999 for chest pains. An angiogram was performed and I was diagnosed as having acid reflux due to stress. There was also some repair done during the procedure.*
- *Loma Linda VAMC Riverside, CA 06/03/2000 (Cellulites). An initial infection set in one of my lower extremities where I was given outpatient Antibiotics, which did not clear the infection.*
- *Loma Linda VAMC Riverside, CA 06/14/2000 (Cellulites). Antibiotics did not work and I was given a second dosage of outpatient Antibiotics, which still did not clear the infection.*
- *Loma Linda VAMC Riverside, CA 07/11 thru 07/17/2000 (Cellulites). I was admitted this time since the infection did not clear up. I additional received meds to take after my stay for an additional 5 days, which are shown on the enclosed medical records.*
- *Las Vegas VAMC 08/06/2000 Another infection set into one of my lower extremities where I was given outpatient Antibiotics and I had to come into the clinic for 3 days and receive IV's of antibiotics. I was then given 10 more days of antibiotics to take at home.*
- *Las Vegas VAMC 07/2002 (Cellulites) I was seen at the Nellis Federal Hospital due to another infection to the lower extremities. I was given outpatient antibiotic for a 7-day period.*
- *Mtn View Hosp Las Vegas, NV 11/09 thru 11/13/2003 (Cellulites & Pneumonia). Admitted due to cellulites infection to the lower extremities and contracting pneumonia. When released I was given additional 5 days of outpatient antibiotics.*
- *NW Medical clinic Las Vegas, NV 01/18/2008 thru 02/21/2008 I had back-to-back cellulites infection. The first I was given antibiotics from the NW Med Clinic, which did not work. I had to eventually go to the emergency room of the Centennial Hospital in Las Vegas where was diagnosed yet again with a cellulites infection to the lower extremities where I was given 2 medications for the infection. Since this attack the bottom of my right heel has become numb. I just finished the last of my antibiotics the week of the 3rd of March 2008.*

In each of the above cases, I was unable to work for at least a 10 to 30 day period. This is an ongoing medical problem that I will have to go through for the rest of my life. The smallest scrap on any portion of my lower extremities will cause an infection and now that my diabetes is hard to control I am really susceptible to even more serious infection.

Conclusion

In 1999, I was diagnosed with diabetes mellitus. In approximately 2005, I became insulin depended. I do feel that had I not had the cold weather injury to my extremities, I would not have contracted diabetes. I would have been able to be more active in my life style. I am not able to do any sports or hard exercises because of my current health. I have enclosed full records for your review. As to my non-VA back injury, I am not able to sit for long period because of pain, which radiate downward through my legs. Being not able to neither stand nor walk for long periods leaves me in a dilemma. I have been offered numerous pain pills by my past and present physicians and have declined the majority of them. Though the pills help somewhat with the pain, I was being left incoherent and confused trying to keep employment and driving. Some of the medications that I take cause constant nausea throughout the day. Especially the blood pressure and insulin meds. My feet and legs are always in some form of pain. Driving causes pain because of my heel problems and back.

I am asking the VA to really look at my records. I appreciate your time and effort in reviewing this request.

End

This was my initial letter requesting a higher rating. The form this information was placed on is VA FORM 21-4138. Now you can clearly see that I mentioned more disabilities that I felt were caused by my cold weather injuries to my lower extremities. When I mentioned diabetes, the RO locked onto that symptom and ran with it and neglected my other injuries accept for the cold injuries to my lower. As I look back on the initial letter, one negative thing that I did was not use the words "secondary, caused or aggravated". This led the Rating board to split my request into two different cases and caused some confusion in the eyes of the Rating Board with what I was exactly seeking. I became a little dismayed that the extra conditions were not seen as a part of my disability but as I researched further into Title 38, I finally realized near the last six months before I actually used the term unemployable, that I did not clearly state my wants. The only thing I can say is make sure in your correspondence to the Rating Board that they know exactly what you are seeking under whatever conditions and if there are conditions that you feel are related to the service injuries that you use the terms "**secondary, caused or aggravated**" correctly. By working with a SR you can save yourself the frustration I went through.

With this first request, I submitted about three inches of medical reports that were required of me to prove my case by March 2008. At this point I had sent actual VA medical records. I had not thought of formatting the form that I want you to use showing dates, location and descriptions of the medical condition you feel are service related. Sending all those documents probably slowed down and hurt my first request. We are going to make sure this does not happen to you.

By April 2008, I decided to contact the VA just to make sure my documents were received. It's a good thing I did because it was stated that the Rating Board had sent a correspondence to me which required a response within sixty days. I stated that I never received it and they faxed me a copy that day. This letter informed me that my file had been received and that it was being worked on. Attached to the letter was a form called VCAA Notice of Response. As mentioned previously, this form gives you the option of deciding your claim with the documents the VA has on hand or sending additional supporting documents that you want the board to review. Also, if there is any missing information the Rating Board needs it would be requested of you in this correspondence. The letter gave me sixty additional days to submit all documents. Of course I went with the additional sixty days. I know each Vet wants to close their case as soon as possible, but you need to make sure you are sending the proper information requested of you and to give time for you to speak with your SR.

The VA requested that I show evidence on my claimed diabetes as well as evidence showing a nexus (connection) between diabetes and my present cold injuries. There was no mention of the other injuries whether they were accepted or not that I felt was service related, so I was lost as to what the RO was actually reviewing. The letter from the VA was about 11 pages. You can review this letter on my website. When you receive any correspondence from the VA, read it very carefully and reply with every item they have requested and do not miss your cutoff date, so make sure it is sent prior to the deadline. As long as the response has been date stamped by a Department of Veterans Affairs Office or service center by the expiration date you are in compliance. Do not wait until the last day. You could take the chance of the VA not receiving it on time. As you read earlier in my letters about my situation where the forms was faxed in and it was supposedly not receive on time, I do not want you to be in the same predicament. Please understand that it will not be an easy process. This can be frustrating sometimes but you have to keep moving forward. This is the main reason why I am trying to streamline the process for you Vets so you do not have to go through what I did.

I sent the Notice of Response back to the VA. In July 2008 there was a request for me to have a C&P (Compensation and Pension) exam. This took place in August 2008.

By November 2008 a decision was rendered on my case stating that my current rating would stay the same and the other requested items were denied. The rating decision **Statement of Case (SOC)** informs you why or why not your case was approved. You can review this document on my website.

Since my initial submission, I had not sent any additional supporting documents. My next step was to respond to the SOC from the Rating Board.

The next letter is my first reply to the SOC correspondence. This typed letter was called a **Notice of Disagreement**. This is basically a hand written letter expressing your concerns about the denial.

Second letter

In response to your decision dated 11/05/2008, I totally disagree with your findings and the Cold Injury Exam performed, which were used in your decision.

These discrepancies are as follows: Par 1
- *Cellulites infection in both lower extremities over the past 10 plus years where the infections entered through my feet and one possibly through my inner thigh.*
- *Numbness of the right great toe*
- *Numbness in heels*
- *Constant pain in both lower extremities to include both feet at all times*
- *Plantar Fasciitis*
- *Tendonitis*
- *Osteoarthritis*
- *Venous insufficiency*
- *Neuropathy in both lower extremities*

In chronological order, below is my argument in regards to the decision made in my case:

- *It is stated that the right and left foot color and affected area were normal. The skin thickness, temperature, and texture were all normal. The hair growth had decreased. There was no fungus and the nails were not affected. There were no callus formations, or infections/ulcerations.*
  - *At the time of the examination I had just completed taking antibiotics to clear up a cellulites infection. Prior to the exam while the infection was in its onset my skin color in the lower extremities were red with the skin shinny and warm to the touch with 2+ edema. One can state at that time my skin would look as if it was thin because of the swelling. From December 2007 through the present I have had 3 to 4 cellulites infection in my lower extremities, which shows in my medical records. Now, where in the decision letter does it show these records where reviewed on my behalf. These are important factors that should have been reviewed since I have cellulites infection constantly and I did mention this in my initial VA Form 21.4138 showing dates and times in the past. Prior to March 2008 I did have callus formation on my heels. An infection that set in on December 2007 and ending in February 2008 entered my body through crack in my heels. At my last diabetes appointment, I was sent to*

dermatology were the doctor explained to me what I had to do in order to minimize the calluses. These records were enclosed also for your review.

- *It is mention that the examiner stated, "He stated that there was some scars 4 mm in diameter". What is not mentioned is that these scars are the entrance wounds where cellulites infections entered my system causing in and out patient stays in multiple private and VA hospitals and clinics. This is information that is very important when analyzing my medical condition to-date and was not addressed.*

- *As to the reflex examination, the examiner did not physically touch my lower extremities to check for pain on manipulation. He did ask where my pain was, which I expressed all the areas to include stiffness.*

- *The decision letter did express that the examiner noticed weakness in the ankles. Again this is a medical condition that should have been reviewed as a functional problem and injury/medical condition related to the cold injury. No weight was given to this statement as describe in Sec 4.40 Functional loss shown below.*

- *Additionally, within the exam and the current decision letter, there is no reference to any of the above listed medical conditions shown in Par 1 of this letter accept the mention of neuropathy, which I feel is misrepresented in your findings. In the decision report beyond the quotes mentioned in your decision "The examiner noted that you have non-services connected diabetes mellitus and non-service connected lumbar spinal stenosis recently diagnosed, which is currently being treated with the possibility of surgery. All of these conditions can cause neuropathy". This was not the examiners complete ending statement. From the exam report it additionally states "Cold weather injury and diabetes mellitus is at least likely as not involving the peripheral nerves and not nerve roots. One cannot resolve this issue without resort to mere speculation: differentiating between residuals of the cold weather injury and any disability superimposed by the NSC back injury and the diabetes". The examiners entire statement should be put into context and not just a portion. By leaving out the examiners ending statement would make one believe that the only possible reason for neuropathy would be caused by diabetes or my back injury. The examiners ending statement clearly states that the neuropathy could have been caused by diabetes, the back injury or the cold weather injury. Under reasonable doubt, one cannot rule out the possibility of the cold injury causing my neuropathy.*

- *As to a higher evaluation of 30%*
    - *I do have constant pain, numbness, and cold sensitivity, color changes and osteoarthritis as required for additional compensation. Beyond the higher evaluation, I have not been considered for lower extremity medical problems such as plantar fasciitis, constant pain in the lower, cellulites, tendonitis, numbness, osteoarthritis nor venous insufficiency per the following rating codes: 5003, 5270, 5271, 5272, 5276, 5278, 5310, 5311, 7113, and 7121.*

I would like to state that the examiner had problems placing information into the program referencing my medical condition. He felt that a lot of the questions were repetitive and with that in mind merely glanced through a large portion of the program. If you notice in the written exam in some areas he stated I had no pain and in others he stated the opposite. He stated he reviewed my full medical records but there were only four records showing on his monitor. I sent records dating from December 1999 through early 2008. My case involving worsening of my condition extends some 10 years plus. All of my past medical history is important in coming to a correct conclusion. This appointment seemed to be more a question and answer session rather than a complete exam by specialized doctors. Since my case involves specialized medical conditions, it is only fair to me that I am allotted to be seen by such doctor. I would request that I be afforded another exam from two medical entities as per my rights based on the following, which I feel was not examined:

TITLE 38--PENSIONS, BONUSES, AND VETERANS' RELIEF
CHAPTER I--DEPARTMENT OF VETERANS AFFAIRS
PART 4-SCHEDULE FOR RATING DISABILITIES--Table of Contents
Subpart B-Disability Ratings

Sec. 4.40 Functional loss: Disability of the musculoskeletal system is primarily the inability, due to damage or infection in parts of the system, to perform the normal working movements of the body with normal excursion, strength, speed, coordination and endurance. It is essential that the examination on which ratings are based adequately portray the anatomical damage, and the functional loss, with respect to all these elements. The functional loss may be due to absence of part, or all, of the necessary bones, joints and muscles, or associated structures, or to deformity, adhesions, defective innervations, or other pathology, or it may be due to pain, supported by adequate pathology and evidenced by the visible behavior of the claimant undertaking the motion. Weakness is as important as limitation of motion, and a part which becomes painful on use must be regarded as seriously disabled. A little used part of the musculoskeletal system may be expected to show evidence of disuse, either through atrophy, the condition of the skin, absence of normal callosity or the like.

Sec. 4.41 History of injury: In considering the residuals of injury, it is essential to trace the medical-industrial history of the disabled person from the original injury, considering the nature of the injury and the attendant circumstances, and the requirements for, and the effect of, treatment over past periods, and the course of the recovery to date. The duration of the initial, and any subsequent, period of total incapacity, especially periods reflecting delayed union, inflammation, swelling, drainage, or operative intervention, should be given close attention. This consideration, or the absence of clear cut evidence of injury, may result in classifying the disability as not of traumatic origin, either reflecting congenital or developmental etiology, or the effects of healed disease.

Sec. 4.42 Complete medical examination of injury cases: The importance of complete medical examination of injury cases at the time of first medical examination by the Department of Veterans Affairs cannot be overemphasized. When possible, this should include complete neurological and psychiatric examination, and other special examinations indicated by the physical condition, in addition to the required general and orthopedic or surgical examinations. When complete examinations are not conducted covering all systems of the body affected by disease or injury, it is impossible to visualize the nature and extent of the service connected disability. Incomplete examination is a common cause of incorrect diagnosis, especially in the neurological and psychiatric fields, and frequently leaves the Department of Veterans Affairs in doubt as to the presence or absence of disabling conditions at the time of the examination.

Sec. 4.45 The joints: As regards the joints the factors of disability reside in reductions of their normal excursion of movements in different planes. Inquiry will be directed to these considerations: (a) Less movement than normal (due to ankylosis, limitation or blocking, adhesions, tendon-tie-up, contracted scars, etc.). (b) More movement than normal (from flail joint, resections, nonunion of fracture, relaxation of ligaments, etc.). (c) Weakened movement (due to muscle injury, disease or injury of peripheral nerves, divided or lengthened tendons, etc.). (d) Excess fatigability. (e) Incoordination, impaired ability to execute skilled movements smoothly. (f) Pain on movement, swelling, deformity or atrophy of disuse. Instability of station, disturbance of locomotion, interference with sitting, standing and weight-bearing are related considerations. For the purpose of rating disability from arthritis, the shoulder, elbow, wrist, hip, knee, and ankle are considered major joints; multiple involvements of the interphalangeal, metacarpal and carpal joints of the upper extremities, the interphalangeal, metatarsal and tarsal joints of the lower extremities, the cervical vertebrae, the dorsal vertebrae, and the lumbar vertebrae, are considered groups of minor joints, ratable on a parity with major joints. The lumbosacral articulation and both sacroiliac joints are considered to be a group of minor joints, ratable
on disturbance of lumbar spine functions .

Sec. 4.57 Static foot deformities. It is essential to make an initial distinction between bilateral flatfoot as a congenital or as an acquired condition. The congenital condition, with depression of the arch, but no evidence of abnormal callosities, areas of pressure, strain or demonstrable tenderness, is a congenital abnormality which is not compensable or pensionable. In the acquired condition, it is to be remembered that depression of the longitudinal arch, or the degree of depression, is not the essential feature. The attention should be given to anatomical changes, as compared to normal, in the relationship of the foot and leg, particularly to the inward rotation of the superior portion of the os calcis, medial deviation of the insertion of the Achilles tendon, the medial tilting of the upper border of the astragalus. This is an unfavorable mechanical relationship of the parts. A plumb line dropped from the middle of the patella falls inside of the normal point. The forepart of the foot is abducted, and the foot everted. The plantar surface of the foot is painful and shows demonstrable tenderness, and manipulation of the foot produces spasm of the Achilles tendon, peroneal spasm due to adhesion about the peroneal sheaths, and other evidence of pain and limited motion. The symptoms should be apparent without regard to exercise. In severe cases there is gaping of bones on the inner border of the foot, and rigid valgus position with loss of the power of inversion and adduction. *Exercise with undeveloped or unbalanced musculature, producing chronic irritation, can be an aggravating factor.* In the absence of trauma or other definite evidence of aggravation, service connection is not in order for pes cavus which is a typically congenital or juvenile disease.

Sec. 4.59 *Painful motion.* *With any form of arthritis, painful motion is an important factor of disability, the facial expression, wincing, etc., on pressure or manipulation, should be carefully noted and definitely related to affected joints.* Muscle spasm will greatly assist the identification. *Sciatic neuritis is not uncommonly caused by arthritis of the spine. The intent of the schedule is to recognize painful motion with joint* or periarticular pathology as productive of disability. *It is the intention to recognize actually painful, unstable, or malaligned joints, due to healed injury, as entitled to at least the minimum compensable rating for the joint. Crepitation either in the soft tissues such as the tendons or ligaments, or crepitation within the joint structures should be noted carefully as points of contact which are diseased. Flexion elicits such manifestations. The joints involved should be tested for pain on both active and passive motion, in weight-bearing and nonweightbearing and, if possible, with the range of the opposite undamaged joint.*

Sec. 4.61 *Examination.* *With any form of arthritis* (except traumatic arthritis) it is essential that the examination for rating purposes cover all major joints, with especial reference to Heberden's or Haygarth's nodes.

Sec. 4.62 *Circulatory disturbances.* *The circulatory disturbances, especially of the lower extremity following injury in the popliteal space, must not be overlooked, and require rating generally as phlebitis.*

Sec. 4.70 *Inadequate examinations.* If the report of examination is inadequate as a basis for the required consideration of service connection and valuation, the rating agency may request a supplementary report from the examiner giving further details as to the limitations of the disabled person's ordinary activity imposed by the disease, injury, or residual condition, the prognosis for return to, or continuance of, useful work. When the *best interests of the service will be advanced by personal conference with the examiner, such conference may be arranged through channels .*

The above etiologies should be looked upon when evaluating my disabilities. Too much enfaces was place on diabetes without including my current declining medical condition referencing my cold weather injuries. In reviewing the current decision under "Evidence", I noticed that the only records reviewed were from September 28, 2007 through September 28, 2008. My submission of documents in March of 2008 to your department extended from December 1999 through roughly March 2008. I am not for sure if your office reviewed these medical documents as they should have been per Sec. 4.41 History of injury, as shown above.

I feel an exam should cover all areas referenced to a person's disability since a person's future depends upon the outcome of an examination. I do not feel I was afforded that comfort at all. Would you not concur? In my mind the exam was not conducted as required by your department or the Cold Weather Protocol for cold injuries. This is not to saying that your examiner was deficient in his duties, but that the exam was incomplete. As to evaluating diabetes, I would request again that I be allotted a specialist in this area to examine me.

I do have additional documentation for submission. So as not to be repetitive, could you please inform me as to the medical file dates in your possession used for the decision letter? Your decision states September 2007 through September 2008. My initial submission covered Dec 1999 through early 2008.

End

The above letter is an example on how I responded to the VA. Again, the only item I would suggest that you change is to only site the section numbers under Title 38 Part 4. I went a little overboard by writing out the entire section but I felt I had to make my case and additionally felt it might be convenient for the RO if they had the definitions of these sections close at hand, though many of them are quite informed or at least have access to the sections. It will not hurt your case if you do decide to add the text. The Rating Board sites these sections when they write you.

Now you see why I said you should really get into reading. If you do not read Title 38 Parts 3 and 4, you could possibly miss out on information that can help your case.
Even though SR's are capable and knowledgeable about Title 38, it is your responsibly to make sure your case is solid.

When you receive correspondences from the Rating Board, they usually site sections from Title 38. Why shouldn't you do the same? These laws can benefit you tremendously if you apply them in a manner that supports your case. Believe me when I say it helps your case. It did for me.

The next correspondence is the third letter and my response to their decision on my Notice of Disagreement. In this letter I ask for a Decision Review Officer (DRO) to review my file. I responded to each statement that was laid out in the VA's decision letter. This let the RO know where I was coming from. Here I submitted additional new and material evidence not submitted earlier to include laymen documentation i.e., medical research reports that I downloaded from the internet, my private fee base podiatrist etiology report and medical records from specialist, VA and private in which I attached to the correspondence. I was repetitive on a few records that I felt was missed, which were very important to my case. By now I was becoming pretty stressed out. I arranged closer appointments with my Mental Health therapist, which really helped. At this point is where I began tinkering around on how to streamline all of my submissions. I decided to format a document that I could use to show medical information without sending a pile of records except those that came from private doctors and imaging centers that I thought were not accessible by the VA. As stated in previous sections, this form allowed me to give dates, places and a brief description of my disabilities on three pages. My plan was to show that I gave the Rating Board specific and sufficient records relating to my disability. My thoughts at the time was If I were to ever have to appeal my case to the BVA, (1) they would see that I meticulously laid out for the Rating Board each supporting record dating back through the most severe time period in which my disabilities began to seriously worsen. I knew that most of the documents that I referenced on my formatted form were already in the hands of the Rating Board, so my intention was to steer the BVA toward reviewing my supporting documents first before they decided what to review on their own. At the same time I could add new evidence on my form for their perusal and have solid proof that I informed the Rating Board of specific record as evidence in supporting my case.

When I made my choice on the type of review I wanted, I personally did not see any reason for me to be present. I stood fast on the premise that my medical documents spoke for themselves. I wanted to make sure my records were actually viewed in the proper context by using their rules of showing a "Nexus" within my disagreement letter stating my condition and how my supportive medical records over the past ten years stated specific connections secondary to my current disability, which were the conditions that I was seeking additional compensation for, also reviewing the history of my injury as stated in Title 38 Part 4 Sec. 4.41 History of injury.

Extremely Important: The above few paragraphs are very important to soak in. When you're stating in a correspondence to the Rating Board that in your medical records they show (depending upon your submission type i.e., new, request for higher rating or appeal) either a condition is caused and/or aggravated or that a condition is secondary to a current service connected injury that those records actually states that. You have no room for error. This statement reflects back throughout this book on how you should review your records to make sure they are descriptive and what you should do if they're not. Now let's look at my third letter.

Third Letter

After reviewing your correspondence dated January 8, 2009, I have decided that a Decision Review Officer should be assigned to my case file for a De Novo review. I know your office is doing its best to assist, but my health is stressing me out. Hopefully, the following response in this letter and the attachments that will be supplied will bring this process to a satisfactory end.

Referencing my past correspondences to your department dated 03/21/2008, 11/08/2008 and 12/16/2008, I am seeking "Total disability ratings for compensation based on unemployability of the individual" and/or a higher rating under Title 38 Part 4 Sec 4.16 and 4.18.

As to the decision of 11/05/2008 I feel it was not conducted properly under Title 38 Part 4 Sections 4.41, 4.42 4.70. Additionally, sections that should be under consideration are 4.40, 4.44, 4.45, 4.57, 4.58, 4.59, 4.61, and 4.62.

Referencing your comments on the nexus between my cold injuries and diabetes, it is just one of the conditions I feel is associated with or aggravates my current cold injuries. Also, the RO did not review my med records concerning other injuries associated with my current status to-date. I also had reservations about my initial med package not being reviewed in its entirety. Per your decision letter, the only documents reviewed were for a 1-year period to-date. My initial package consisted of material dating from early 1998 through March 2008. These periods would have covered from my first initial combined rating of 40% to the present and would show my condition deteriorating.

Sec. 1
In order to assist you in your review, I'm referencing dates of med records that show a nexus between my cold weather injuries and the listed disabilities shown in Sec 1a and medical research reports printed from online medical sites such as, MayoClinic.com and Vascular Web. Any new and material evidence not submitted prior are enclosed with this correspondence.

1a. Additional Injuries

- Constant pain in lower extremities
- Chronic Lymphedema (bilateral)
- Chronic Venous Insufficiency (bilateral)
- Chronic Cellulites
- Edema
- PVD/PAD
- Neuropathy lower extremities (bilateral)
- Numbness of the right great toe and heels
- Fatigue
- Plantar Fasciitis/Heel Spurs private Dr Mark Brenis,
- Flatfeet/Hammer toes
- Hammertoes
- Tendonitis
- Osteoarthritis/arthritis (ankles and knees)
- Phlebitis
- Hypertension
- Diabetes Mellitus (insulin dependent)
- Sciatic nerve problem

Sec. 2 Medical record dates to be reviewed

2a. Non-VA care facilities

- *10/24/98-11/06/98* (cellulites) hospitalized private hospital Salinas Valley Hosp and outpatient treatment
- *11/16/98* (cellulites) further antibiotics out-patient private MD R. Abundis
- *01/26/99* Plantar Fasciitis/Heel Spurs private podiatric Mark Brenis
- *02/05/99* private R. Abundis, MD stop working letter
- *11/03/99* Electromyogram

2b. VA facilities

- *02/99 thru 11/99* seen multiple MD's at Ft Ord, CA for lower extremity problems. Should be in C-file. Also water therapy and mental health for depression
- *11/19/99* Orthopedic Clinic - Chronic lymphedema secondary to frostbite
- *12/02/99 thru 12/13/99* Fitted for prosthetics and physical exam with new VA doctor
- *03/07/00* X-rays

Lymphedema (this is where my treatment treatment stopped for some time (very bad situation for me). I should have been offered more help
- *07/02 thru 10/03* I'm not sure what my status was. Records should be in C-file
- *11/10/03* Private hospital Mountain View cellulites in-patient
- *12/03 thru 05/05* I'm not sure what my status was. Records should be in C-file
- *05/23/05* Cellulites -

status was
- *01/18/08 thru 02/26/08* cellulites infection
- *02/29/08* Dermatology
- *05/14/08* Peripheral Neuropathy
- *06/03/08* Bilateral lower extremity Venous Doppler and Arterial Doppler Ultrasound
- *08/08 thru present* Private podiatrist (Foot, Ankle & lower Leg Center)

private neurologist R. Lawrence, MD
- *11/03/99* private MD Electromyogram S1 radiculopathy
- *11/10/03 thru 11/23/03* cellulites inpatient private Mountain View Hosp and 10 days extra antibiotics

- *03/09/00* Podiatry Clinic Infection not cleared
- *03/14/00* Neurology Dept
- *04/18/00* Dermatology
- *06/03/00* ER Loma Linda VAMC cellulites

chronic lymphedema
- *08/29/05* Numbness in feet
- *09/15/05* EMG/NCS of bilateral legs
- *09/15/05 thru 12/07* I'm not sure what my
- *08/26/08* C & P Exam
- *09/10/08* Prosthetics night splints
- *10/01/08* cellulites Infections 10 days antibiotics

- *10/06/08* follow-up cellulites infection
- *10/23/08* thru present Private therapy clinic (Advanced Manual Therapy Institute *01/15/09* MRI lower extremities
- *01/26/09* PAC Clinic PAD 3000 vascular microlabratory test

Sec 3
The above records are the only ones in my possession. I did request a copy of my C-file in order to fill in the gaps, but have not received them as yet. These records shows that Sec. 1a above is secondary to my service connected cold weather injuries.

Sec 4
Below are brief excerpt from attached research reports showing a nexus between my medical complications.

4a. Foot pain: Most foot pain is due to poorly fitting shoes, injuries and overuse. But **structural defects and conditions such as diabetes** *and* **arthritis** *also* **can lead to foot problems**. *Common causes of foot pain include:* **Achilles tendinitis, Achilles tendon rupture, Bone spurs, Diabetic neuropathy, Flatfeet, Hammertoe and mallet toe, Ingrown toenails, Osteoarthritis, Peripheral neuropathy, Plantar fasciitis, Poor posture or postural defects.**

4b. Chronic Lymphedema: **Swelling to** *arm and* **legs** *when blockage in your* **lymphatic system** *prevents the* **lymph fluid from draining properly**. *The lymphatic system assist in carrying waste product by way of through* **lymph vessels**, *which lead to* **lymph nodes**. *Waste is then filtered out by* **lymphocytes. Bacteria** *can lead to* **cellulites infections**.

4c. Edema: Edema occurs when tiny blood vessels in your body (capillaries) leak fluid. The **fluid** *from the capillaries leaks into the surrounding tissue, causing the* **tissue to swell**. *In some cases, however,* **edema** *may be a sign of a more serious underlying* *medical condition. Diseases and conditions that may cause edema include: Congestive heart failure, Cirrhosis, Kidney disease, Kidney damage,* **Weakness or damage to veins in your legs such as, Chronic venous insufficiency,** *and* **Inadequate lymphatic system. Certain medication can cause edema such as, nonsteroidal anti-inflammatory drugs (NSAIDs),** *estrogens and certain* **diabetes medications called thiazolidinediones — can increase your risk of edema.**

4d. Chronic Venous Insufficiency (CVI): The **flow** *of oxygen rich* **blood** *from your heart to the rest of your body, which in turn veins return oxygen poor blood back to the heart.* **CVI may cause swelling of the lower extremities, calves may feel tight, legs can feel heavy, tired, restless, or achy and the feeling of pain when walking. Legs can swell** *due to your* **lymphatic system producing fluid,** *called* **lymph,** *to compensate for CVI. Leg tissues may absorb some of the fluid,* **which can increase the tendency for legs to swell.**

4e. Chronic Cellulites: **Lower extremities is the most commonly affected area. It appears as swollen, red area of the skin that feels hot and tender.** *It can enter when one or more types of* **bacteria enters through a crack, break in the skin or some type of trauma. Age can be a factor** *because of your* **circulatory system** *becomes less affective at delivering blood with infection fighting cells to some area of the body.* **Diabetes** *impairs the* **immune system** *and increases the risk of* **infections. Chronic swelling of the lower extremities (lymphedema)** *may crack leaving the skin vulnerable to* **bacterial infection.** *Various factors increase the risk of recurrent cellulites, including:* **Breaks in the skin, Chronic skin conditions, Chronic lymphedema, Poor circulation, and Weak immune system**

4f. PVD/PAD: While there are many causes of peripheral vascular disease, doctors commonly use the term peripheral vascular disease to refer to peripheral artery disease (peripheral arterial disease, PAD). **PVD/PAD usually affects your lower extremities.** *When there is not enough* **blood flow, most notable symptoms are leg pains when walking.** *PVD/PAD can lead to* **open sores** *that don't heel,* **injury,** *or* **infection of the feet and legs, such as cellulites** *especially having diabetes.*

4g. Peripheral Neuropathy: PVD/PAD **causes pain and numbness in your hands and feet.** *PVD/PAD can result from* **traumatic injuries, infections, metabolic problems** *and exposure to toxins. One of the most common causes is* **diabetes.**

4h. Plantar Fasciitis: **Heel pain** *caused by* **inflammation** *of the* **plantar fascia. Plantar fasciitis** *causes* **stabbing or burning pain.** *The cause for plantar fascia can be from* **physical activity overload, arthritis, diabetes, flat foot, or other weight bearing activities.**

4i. Flatfeet/Hammer toes: While flatfeet usually won't cause any problems, **if the condition causes your ankles to turn inward, you may have problems in your feet, ankles and knees.** *An overload to this tendon can cause* **inflammation of the tendon (tendinitis)** *and even* **tearing of the tendon.** *Once the* **tendon** *is* **damaged** *the foot's arch loses support and can flatten.*

4j. Tendinitis: Tendinitis is **inflammation or irritation of a tendon.** *If tendinitis is severe and leads to the* **rupture of a tendon,** *you may need surgical repair. But many times, rest and medications to reduce the pain and* **inflammation** *of* **tendinitis** *may be the only treatments you need.* **If tendinitis is severe and leads to the rupture of a tendon, you may need surgical repair.** *But many times, rest and medications to reduce the pain and* **inflammation of tendinitis** *may be the only treatments you need.* **The most common cause of tendinitis is injury or overuse** *during work or play. The pain is usually the result of a* **small tear in or inflammation** *of the tendon that links your muscle to your bone.*

4k. Osteoarthritis: **Osteoarthritis,** *sometimes called* **degenerative joint disease** *or* **osteoarthrosis,** *is the most common form of* **arthritis.** *Osteoarthritis occurs when* **cartilage** *in your* **joints** *wears down over time. Osteoarthritis can affect any* **joint in your body,** *though it* **most commonly affects** *joints in your hands, hips,* **knees and spine.** *Osteoarthritis is a degenerative disease that* **worsens over time.** *As many as a third of people with osteoarthritis will eventually* **experience significant disability.** **Joint pain and stiffness may become severe enough to make getting through the day difficult, if not impossible. Some people are no longer able to work.**

4l. Phlebitis: Thrombophlebitis (throm-bo-fluh-BI-tis) occurs when a **blood clot causes swelling in one or more of your veins, typically in your legs.** *When a vein close to the surface of your skin is affected, you may see a red, hard and tender cord just under the surface of your skin.* **When a deep vein in the leg is affected, your leg may become swollen, tender and painful, most noticeably when you stand or walk.** *You may also have* **a fever.** *However, many people with deep vein thrombosis have no symptoms.*

4m. Diabetes Mellitus: In type 1 diabetes, your **immune system** *— which normally fights harmful* **bacteria** *or viruses — attacks and destroys the insulin-producing cells in the pancreas. This leaves you with little or no insulin. Instead of being transported into your cells, sugar builds up in your bloodstream.* **The exact cause of type 1 diabetes is unknown.** *Peripheral neuropathy is the most common form of diabetic neuropathy. It* **damages nerves in your feet, legs,** *arms and hands,* **but your legs and feet are affected most often.** *Symptoms include:* **Peripheral neuropathy** *is the most common form of diabetic neuropathy. Symptoms include:* **numbness,** *a* **tingling, burning or prickling sensation that starts in your toes or the balls of your feet and gradually spreads** *upward, sharp, jabbing or electric shock-like pain that's worse at night, extreme sensitivity to the lightest touch* — for some people, even the **weight of a sheet can be agonizing, loss of balance** and **coordination, muscle weakness and difficulty walking, and serious foot problems,** such as ulcers, **infections, deformities,** and bone and **joint pain.**

4n. Sciatic nerve problem: The sciatic nerve r**uns from your spinal cord to your buttock and hip area and down the back of each leg. You can experience pain likely to occur along a path from your low back to your buttock and the back of your thigh and calf, numbness or muscle weakness along the nerve pathway in your leg or foot. In some cases, you may have pain in one part of your leg and numbness in another and tingling or a pins-and-needles feeling, often in your toes or part of your foot.**

4o. Frostbite: Although anyone who is exposed to freezing cold for a prolonged period of time can get frostbite, people who are taking beta-blockers, which decrease the flow of blood to the skin, are particularly susceptible. So are people with **peripheral vascular disease** *(a disorder of the arteries). Other things that may increase the risk of frostbite include: smoking, windy weather (which increases the rate of heat loss from skin),* **diabetes, peripheral neuropathy,** *and Raynaud's phenomenon.*

This concludes the first portion of my request. The balance of the correspondence deals with Title 38 Part 4 Sec 4.29. I am seeking past and present compensation based on Title 38 Part 4 Sec 4.29 "Ratings for service-connected disabilities requiring hospital treatment or observation".

My initial stay in a hospital for cellulites infections was approximately 1982, which the exact date would show in my C-file at Ft Miley VA Med Hosp San Francisco, CA. I stayed in the hospital for approximately 4-5 days for infection to my lower extremities. After my release I was given an additional x 10 days worth of antibiotics. I was incapacitated for 45 days.

- Salinas Valley Memorial (SMV) Hosp Salinas, CA (Cellulites). An initial infection set in on 03/98. Antibiotics were given and the infection subsides for a few months. On 10/20/1998 thru 11/07/1998 I was hospitalized with cellulites for 4 days and then released on an outpatient bases with assistance from VNA for an additional 10 days of IV antibiotics. I was then placed on deep-water therapy for 3 months under the care of R. Abundis, MD and M. Brenis, podiatrist until the end of February 1999. During this period of treatment and observation I was unable to work. Dr. Abundis actually felt I should stop working all together and wrote a letter to that fact. My C-file should have medical documents reflecting these dates. Throughout the balance between February

1999 thru May 2000, multiple VA doctors were observing me for my condition. Again these file are in my C-file.

06/03/2000 cellulites set into my lower extremities again. I went to the ER at Loma Linda VAMC in Riverside, CA where I was treated on an outpatient basis and given antibiotic x 10 days. The infection did not clear and I went back to the same ER and was given additional antibiotics on an outpatient basis. Again, I had to return to the same ER when was admitted and stayed from 07/11/2000 thru 07/17/2000. When released I was given antibiotics x 10 days and was told to follow up with a physician once I arrived in Las Vegas. When moving to Las Vegas in August 2000, I again had a cellulites attack and was treated at the Las Vegas VAMC on 08/06/2000 and was again given intravenous antibiotics up until 08/09/2000. Once that was completed I was given antibiotics x 10 days on an outpatient bases. I was treated throughout the rest of the year at the Las Vegas VAMC. I attempted to work for a short 3-month period toward the latter part of the year but my lower extremity problem stopped me with chronic lymphedema. I also attempted to complete a distant education class on a full time basis but again my cold injuries prevented me and I was told to cut down on my studies, which a letter from my doctor was presented to the college (Bellevue Community College).

From 07/18/01 thru 11/03 I had multiple cellulites infections on an outpatient basis, which left me home bound for periods over 30 on each occasion. Each infection I would receive antibiotic x 10 days plus because of the lymphedema and phlebitis that existed after each infection.

Las Vegas VAMC 07/05/2002 (Cellulites) I was seen at the Nellis Federal Hospital due to another infection to the lower extremities. I was given outpatient antibiotic for a 7-day period. Thereafter I was given an additional x 10 days of antibiotics from the Las Vegas VAMC. I was incapacitated for at least 45 days plus due to excess swelling and pain in my lower extremities.

Be advised, that on 07/22/02 I was sent to VA Physical therapy by my VA podiatrist for chronic lymphedema. This is where my treatment stopped. Quoting the therapist "there is nothing further RO can offer this RO at this time" (very bad situation for me). I should have been offered more help through a private podiatrist at that time if there was nothing else the VA could do for me.

On 11/10/03 I was admitted to a private hospital (Mountain View) for a 4-day period for cellulites and pneumonia. I had a panic attack from being in the hospital and was released on the fourth day. I received antibiotics on an outpatient basis to take home x 10 days. My primary physician monitored me at the time.

At Centennial Hospital, Las Vegas, NV 01/18/08 thru 02//26/08 (Cellulites) back-to-back cellulites infections to the lower extremities. Given antibiotics on an outpatient basis and referred to my primary doctor for additional antibiotics x 10 days. This was the last time I was employed. Between this period and up until I contracted another cellulites infection in 05/08 I have been monitored by my primary doctor for chronic lymphedema. In 10/08 I contracted another cellulites infection as was given antibiotics x 10 days.

From 08/18/2008 until the present, I have been under the care (on an out-patient basis) with the Foot, Ankle & Lower Leg Center undergoing therapy. In addition to this clinic, they sent me to Advance Manual Therapy Institute from 10/18/2008. to present for physical therapy. These reports are in my C-file plus I am attaching to this correspondence additional reports.

As you can see, I have never really had a chance to recover from any of these infections. Had I known about Title 38 Part 4 Sec 4.29 and the compensation I am entitled to, I would have submitted the proper request many years ago. Unless a veteran knows about Title 38, they will never know what benefits are avail to them because no VA entity notifies hospitalized vets. The veteran's hospitals never approach me to inform about such benefits. I should not be penalized because of this and the VA hospital system should be held responsible. This might sound harsh but it is my true feelings.

All med records should be in my C-file. Again, I have attempted to get copies with no avail. Should you need additional information, feel free to contact ma at your leisure.

End

As you can see, I am not shy about expressing my concerns. If you do not tell them what you feel is wrong, they have nothing to go off of when reviewing your file. You should also notice some of the verbiage I used. I tried to keep in sync with medical terminology. To me it is showing that you have done your homework.

The outcome of this correspondence was negative. Again I was turned down, so I decided to request for a BVA video conference. At the same time I began to send letters to President Obama, Secretary of the Army Shinseki, the Senator and Governor of Nevada and Congresswomen Dina Titus. I sent each one of these individuals a copy of all correspondents that I had sent the Rating Board. Needless to say all department responded accept Secretary Shinseki. Within weeks I began receiving correspondences from the above and the Rating Board and shortly thereafter I received my 90% rating to include unemployability benefits. There was no need for a BVA hearing so it was cancelled.

My intentions for writing to all of the political powers were to get the Rating Board to fully review all of my medical record. I was confident that if I could get someone to really review my case that the medical records would speak for themselves and it finally did. It makes you wonder if I eventually received my current rating after three years why did I not get it from the beginning. I plan on sending a request to the Regional office to show me how my case was reviewed and what led to their decision. I'll keep you updated on the response on my website once I receive a response. You can review my existing approval on my website.

Know you should have a good grasp on what it will take to submit a good sound case file to the VA. This information is not made up. This is actually how I received my current status of 90% combined rating with a 100% unemployability status.

If there are any questions that you have, pleases go to my website and email your question and I will do my best to answer them.

Good Luck

www.ingramcontent.com/pod-product-compliance
Lightning Source LLC
Chambersburg PA
CBHW081543040426
42448CB00015B/3210